GOING

THROUGH THE

GARDEN

RONELLA STAGNER

Best wishes and
Good Gardening!
Ronella Stagner
5-21-08

Printed by:

Lighthouse PUBLISHING, INC.
Phone: (423) 447-3567
14377 Old St. Hwy. 28 ◆ Pikeville, TN 37367
E-mail: info@lighthousepublishing.org

www.lighthousepublishing.org

INTRODUCTION

When I was a small child, there was no television, no movies and no radio. I lived with my parents about two miles from my grandparents, my Ma and Pa. I developed a very special bond with my wonderful grandmother at a very early age and spent as much time with her as my parents would allow. When my father could stand it no longer, he would ride his horse to Ma's and put me up in front of the saddle and take me home. I had a baby sister and felt that Ma's was a better place to be.

From following her every step, I learned to love flowers as she did. She talked constantly as she worked, about her plants and life in general, and I learned about plants before I learned my ABC's. She had many flowers at the old house, some of which her mother-in-law had planted. I learned which plants needed shade, which needed more water, etc. I helped carry buckets of chicken manure, tobacco stalks and water to her flowers. I was always allowed to pick a bouquet from her gardens to grace the old dining table.

I am often asked how I remember the different plants and their needs and I like to compare myself with the little boys who know every famous baseball player and all the stats.

This sweet, loving woman lived to be very old and visited me at my own home many times where she marveled at the new varieties of roses, phlox, bulbs and other plants. She was also intrigued by the insect sprays and fertilizers.

Ma was essentially a lover of beauty and created beauty in her surroundings, whether in her flower beds, her quilts or in her immaculate old house. When I see a particularly beautiful white lily or a special rose, I think of Ma. As you read this book I hope you learn to appreciate my wonderful grandmother.

—Ronella Stagner

My grandmother,
Sally Lewis

CONTENTS

Dedication

To Amy Wallace Brack who helped me with this book in so many ways.

To the memory of Sally Hall Lewis, my wonderful grandmother, who taught me so much about gardening and about life in general.

To the many readers, who have encouraged me with my weekly columns.

JANUARY

The holidays are behind us and it's time to start thinking of gardening for the new year.

If you failed to get some tulips planted in November, it's not too late. It happens to the best of us. Pick a day or two when the temperature rises enough to make digging easy and plant them now. Always remember to plant with the pointy side up. If planted upside down, tulips will somehow grow as they should but will be late with strange looking tops.

While on the subject of tulips, did you know that the Dutch outlawed the bulb trade during World War II and tulip farmers became so desperate for food that they resorted to eating the tulip bulbs to keep from starving? Did you know that you must feed tulip bulbs with a balanced bulb food at planting time and just after they bloom? Did you also know that you must not cut those yellowing rotting leaves after the tulips have bloomed? They may not bloom again if you do. That's why it's best to plant tulips as an under planting with spring perennials like daylilies. Those begin to show just as tulips are dying. Some gardeners have trouble with squirrels eating the tulip bulbs. There are a couple of easy remedies. One is to dig the required planting hole, cover the bulbs with chicken wire and then cover with dirt. One old gardener dipped the bulbs in cayenne pepper before planting. This seemed to work for him. The biggest reason for tulips not blooming are overwatering and overfeeding. They will pretty much care for themselves if planted in a good soil and not over mothered.

The above tulip information comes to this gardener's mind while looking out of a frosted window at a white world.

Begin to check your young trees at intervals to be sure that some rabbit isn't making a dinner of the tender bark. You can buy a very handy covering which just locks in place or you can buy a wrap. Rodents also can kill young trees in a hurry.

Now is a good time to plant a holly tree. There are so many varieties with different needs so ask your nurseryman for advice. If you want one with dark green leaves all winter and red berries, he can give you the right plant. If you are trying to decide where to plant it, let me recommend a spot where you and your family can enjoy it, such as the front yard. Use it as a specimen plant but be sure that you know how big it will grow before you plant.

On a warm winter day, when you can't stand not getting out into the garden, consider digging up your garden. Not when it's frozen or wet! Here are some benefits from doing this chore in January. First, you expose the soil to freezing and thawing which breaks up clods. The turning also exposes eggs of many insects to the effects of the sun, wind, freezing and the food-hunting birds all of which help to thin the ranks of insects. When spring comes, you are one jump ahead of at least some of the pests.

It's a wise person who only makes New Year's resolutions which are easy to keep. I think every gardener starts making plans or resolutions each January. When the new catalogs start coming, most of us start thinking of what went wrong last summer and what we would like to add. It may be a water garden or a container garden or just another big flower bed. But January is the time for getting materials lined up.

Many gardeners prefer container gardening once they try it. A container garden is simply a collection of flowers grown in pots of various kinds and clumped together to make a garden. These pots can be easily moved around to take advantage of sun or shade. Another advantage is that they move easily if the gardener moves to another location.

Container gardening is a great way to have flowers around a back door, a deck or in some dull corner, especially if the soil is rocky or poor. If this kind of gardening strikes your fancy, you will need time to buy the pots. I have a friend who grows everything in pots that I grow in flower beds, including perennials and bulbs.

January is a good time to plan the flowers you want to add rather than waiting until spring and buying the wrong plants when choosing in a hurry.

Another good item to buy or make now is stakes for those tall perennials. They are a necessary part of gardening and we usually think of them last. Plants should be staked when only a few inches high. You can buy metal or bamboo stakes or make your own as many of us do. A small furniture maker or any carpenter or even a sawmill will have scraps just right for staking. Cut them into various lengths, lay them out on newspaper in the yard or garden shed and spray them with green paint, turn them over when dry and spray again. These stakes will blend into the background of your beds and will last for several years if taken up each fall and stored in a dry place.

Buy your seeds early to start those indoor flats of annuals which have a long germination period because the traditional time for planting them is about February 22. I don't know why that date is set but it has just evolved as THE DAY. It's like St. Patrick's Day is the time to trim roses the final time. Some annuals that should be started this early are lobelia, ageratum, petunia, penstemon, scabosia and a few others.

If you failed to fertilize your lawn in the fall, you can fertilize very lightly at the end of January. Use the usual high-nitrogen fertilizer and stand back and watch that grass grow in March.

If you raise buddleas, prune them this month. Cut them back to 6 inches. All flowers on buddleas, or butterfly bush, bloom on new growth this spring and summer so you aren't cutting any flowering branches. In fact, what you are doing when you cut them back is making the shrub bushier and fuller. If you lose a butterfly bush, it isn't because you trimmed it back but because we, in Kentucky, live at the uppermost climate range for this plant and in Northern Kentucky, if you have one that lives and blooms, you are lucky or maybe you're good!

It's really a Southern plant but I think it's worth the gamble of losing one or two now and then. I had a beautiful pink that made it through two winters and died on the third.

Are you thinking of those lush tomatoes you are going to grow this year? Why not make some plans? Save egg shells and make a mote around each tomato plant of the crushed egg shells to discourage cut worms. And did you know that alyssum planted near your tomato vines will attract the insects which pollinate the tomato plants and they give you bigger crops. On the other hand, marigolds planted near tomatoes will repel insects. Crushed marigold leaves and blooms added to a sprayer can (not your pump sprayer) will make a good spray to repel insects. Of course this washes off with each rain. But the point is there are good plants for your vegetable garden and bad plants to have there.

If you have bananas that get too ripe to use, throw them in the freezer in any old kind of plastic bag and use them this spring around your roses and other perennials. One to each plant gives them a big spurt of energy. Never throw away a banana or the skins. Truly, they make a difference.

The smelly yarrow makes a great addition to compost heaps because they act as a compost activator. I have always had the huge yellow yarrow because I like to dry it and when a stem was cut back, I just automatically put in on the compost, little knowing that it was good for composting. Another great addition to the center of your compost heap is fresh manure because it really heats up the whole heap. Freshly cut grass does the same thing.

A little planning before spring can cut down on your spraying in the flower garden and also the vegetable garden. Does your garden have a lot of lady wigs or lady bugs? Some of us have too many and they invade the inside of your house. They are great to have in the garden as is the great friend of gardeners, the praying mantis. The mantis is such an ugly creature but is the best thing you can have in the garden. You can order them if you wish from most any really good garden catalog. I have been fortunate to find one every now and then. That's because he's so well camouflaged that you may not even know he's there and just occasionally see one.

It's kind of like someone told me about my garter snakes: if you only see one, you can be sure there are dozens more just well hid. That makes me feel really good about working among my plants.

This same fountain of snake lore told me that Trigg and Calloway Counties are the only counties in Kentucky with pigmy rattlesnakes. To make me feel a little better, he told me that the pigmy rattlesnakes are found only in wooded areas and that's where I'm not likely to be found so I felt better.

Spray your evergreens now to keep down the red spider as well as scale and other pests. Check with your local gardening store for the best spray. Also, very carefully shake off any snow which clings to your evergreens since the shape of your plants can be spoiled beyond remedy if snow is left on them.

It's also time to prune your fruit trees. They will bear much better if they are pruned correctly and the best info comes from your local County Agent. My dear old grandfather had a wonderful, very old orchard with every kind of fruit. A great old fellow came around every year to carefully prune each tree and they had been bearing for many, many years.

Soap and water work wonders with dust-clogged leaf pores of house plants. Most potted plants like to get their moisture, as do their outdoor relatives, by drinking with their roots from below.

Use a deep saucer in which to stand each pot for at least an hour. Try to keep your houseplants from being exposed to cold drafts from doors opening. Remember to do your watering in the morning and let the foliage be dry by night. Don't water on a regular basis, like once a week. Each plant has its own needs and there are so many variables like the heat in the room, the amount of sunlight, the kind of pot, etc. When the soil feels dry to the touch, it's time to water. As for feeding, most plants like to rest from October through May so hold the food. The bloomers, like the African violets, need to be fed on a regular basis with their own special fertilizer. Please don't use the Miracle Grow that you use outside. Won't work. When you are watering, check for those tiny insects and disease. There are insecticides made for houseplants which are safe to use indoors. To identify the pesky invader, you will need a good book on houseplants, which I hope you got for Christmas. I have come to the conclusion that growing houseplants is all just trial and error and some plain old luck.

This is a good time to repot your root-bound ferns, the asparagus or others. You will know they are potbound when they seem to have stopped growing and take up water immediately. You can grow the divisions through the winter and even surprise friends with a nice gift. A pot-bound fern will have roots climbing all over the inside of the pot in a white mass. Cut the root ball in halves or quarters from top to bottom. Use a sharp knife and make clean cuts.

Untangle the roots so they will spread out in the new pot. Place a few inches of soil in the pot and spread the roots over it. Fill in the rest, watering as you go. Needless to say, use very good, sterile potting soil.

Remember last year when you resolved to get those lawn mowers tuned and the blades sharpened before mowing time? When you take your mowers to be sharpened, don't forget to take extra blades as well. Remember those shops will be very busy this spring.

Speaking of mowers, did you know that the first motor-driven lawn mower was invented in 1902 by an Englishman and leave it to the American inventors, it was an American who attached a gasoline motor from his washing machine to his hand mower and started manufacturing "Moto-Mowers".

The first rotary mowers were developed in the 1930's. Then followed all kinds of motor driven tools for the gardener, including electric edgers, weedeaters, etc. And now you can call a service which will do all lawn care for you. Wonder what's next.

I remember when my grandfather mowed the big front yard with a mule drawn mower. I wasn't allowed to go near the yard because occasionally a snake would be cut up by the blades. At home, I thought the push-mower a most wonderful thing and could hardly wait to get big enough to push that mower. Strangely, I never have gotten big enough to mow!

❀   ❀   ❀   ❀

I hope you have many bird houses or are making some. A little knowledge of the nesting needs of the most familiar types of birds will keep them safe from their enemies. Please don't make the mistake we made with bluebird houses. We put one on a fence post at our new house long ago. We had dear Sam, a much beloved cat, but since he didn't seem interested as they made their nest, we quit worrying. Smart Sam! He waited until there were little birds in the nest, climbed easily up the wooden post and devoured the whole bunch of babies. We soon knew where to put the bird houses.

A metal sheet tacked around bird house poles will keep cats from climbing. Wood makes the best bird houses and keeps the colors very somber if you must paint them. Each year they want to return to a clean house so that's your job. Just leave some nesting materials nearby. They like to make their own nests, thank you! Some great nesting materials are lint from your dryer, some straw and some old rag scraps as sewers have in abundance. I have heard of some strange things found in bird nests. One thing they seem to like is piles of hair from the barber. Another is bits of string or rubber bands. You know of other things, I'm sure.

The Purple Martin, the largest of the swallows, is the only bird who likes communal living. They like a porch without a railing where they can sun themselves. They arrive in April and nest in May and stay until September and are the most valuable of birds. They will nest in gourds but only if you string them on a wire between trees and in the sun. They will not nest in a house in a tree. They come swooping into their nest and want nothing between them and their nest.

The Wren will build in most anything and most anywhere but their entrance must be no larger than 7/8 inch or cats can get to their young. This size also keeps out the sparrows. Poor sparrows! Someone is always trying to keep out the sparrows.

The Robin likes a sheltered shelf, open on three sides such as a board nailed under the eaves. It is the best known and most sociable of all the birds and will build where no other bird will build. Give him pieces of apple, suet, unsalted meat scraps or crumbs and he will perch on your porch railing. His big preference is cherries. You can't raise cherry trees and court the Robin. My grandmother put up huge nets to keep out birds, mostly Robins which she hated. That one cherry tree, old and crooked, was a prized possession and she and I worked hard to keep the birds from eating her cherries. My job was to climb up into the tree and help get the net over it. Ma could make wonderful things with those cherries.

You may have heard that you shouldn't feed the birds if you're not going to continue on a regular basis. You can just ignore that bit of nonsense. When the snow blankets the countryside, they have no place to find food. Many birds starve each winter. If you don't have bird feeders, just put bird food under a tree or near shrubs where they are staying to keep warm. Or you could scatter food under your window so you can watch them feed. Please feed them a good quality food, not bread scraps alone. Various millets should be the main part of wild bird food.

The following are some more facts about wild birds. The Bluebird will nest in a swinging house and a Sparrow won't. Since the Sparrow is the Bluebird's worst enemy, this is important. It may not be important to you, but sure is to the Bluebird. The Sparrow will actually drive a Bluebird away when he is trying to build a nest. Have the nest in place for Bluebirds by March 5th since the bird nests in early April. I raised some gourds several years ago just for Bluebirds. I hung them in a mulberry tree and waited. For 2 years, I waited and finally one built a nest and they have been coming to those gourds every year. You need to cut a small hole in the bottom of the gourd and affix a little stick of some kind to the hole because they like a roosting place before going in.

All bird houses except the Martin's should have partial shade and all need a number of ¼ inch holes just under the eaves for ventilation.

A wonderful thing you can do for birds in winter is to roll a pine cone in peanut butter and then bird seed and place it in the branches of a shrub. You can hang it by a string or just put in the fork of a branch.

If you are interested in feeding birds this winter, the following is a wonderful, easy recipe which gives them everything they need and also seems to be what they want. Start with 10 pounds plain flour. Then melt about seven cups of lard and three cups peanut butter. Mix gradually with the dry flour. It should be fairly firm. Add raisins, cracked peanuts and whatever else you choose. In the spring, add crushed egg shells. Pack the mixture in pans and put in the freezer until firm enough to cut into strips that will fit in your feeder. Once they are cut, store in the freezer until they are hard, and then put them in plastic bags to store in the freezer till needed.

If you're interested in directions for building bird houses, write to Superintendent of Documents, Government Printing Office, Washington, D.C. and ask for a copy of Bulletin 1456, "Homes for Birds". Or I'm sure they have a web site.

One thing which is such a pleasure for the gardener in January is to force early flowering trees and shrubs to bloom indoors. The forsythia, which I really don't appreciate at its usual blooming time, looks mighty good on a cold January day. Some easy shrubs to force are Flowering Almonds, Bridal Wreath, Japonica and Spirea. Just bring in some branches, put them in a vase of warm water and wait for flower buds.

It's time to start saving dryer lint to put out for building material for birds this spring. I like to save coffee grounds and banana peels in the freezer to put just under the soil around roses. Sometimes, I forget that I put that stuff in the freezer and wonder for a few seconds what this messy looking bag could be.

Save your plastic milk jugs, cut off the bottom and you have a mini-greenhouse for those early vegetables. Or remove the cap, cut off the bottom and bury the jug upside down next to a squash or pumpkin hill for fast, deep watering. Just fill the funnel and let the water trickle down while you do something else. Works for any plant with deep roots. You can use the bottom third of a jug for seed starter trays.

FEBRUARY

The north wind doth blow and we shall have snow,
And what shall poor Robin do then, poor thing?
He'll hide in the barn to keep himself warm
And hide his head under his wing, poor thing.

The above is an old song which my mother sang to me as a wee child and I think of it often at this time of the year. Back then, I looked far into the dark rafters of the big barn thinking to see a Robin huddling on a rafter in the cold. Strange what ideas are imprinted on children.

Maybe the gardener feels that this month is a long time before the busy spring but it isn't so long. March, which is our busiest month, is just around the corner. Anything which you can do now to

21

lessen the chores in the month of March, by all means do it.

The time for selecting annual seeds is at hand. For all round general use and beauty, nothing can equal petunias, marigolds, nasturtiums, zinnias and snapdragons. Many of those old favorites come in a great variety of colors and shapes, especially the old stand-by, the zinnia, which comes in sizes such as the tiny Lilliput to the great dahlia-flowered one. It would take a whole column and then some to do justice to the lowly zinnia. The versatile zinnia does best when intermingled with plants of softer foliage texture. These old favorites are the ones which withstand all kinds of mistreatment and come up looking great.

If you haven't ordered your flower seeds and studied your shrubbery needs, February is the time to do it while you have the leisure time to let ideas rattle around in your mind and be sure that it is the thing you want to do. Most gardens are spoiled by snap decisions made in the heat of a busy season. And by the way, don't forget to include shipping in your order.

Sponge the leaves of house plants every week with clean water. Give them plenty of fresh air, but no drafts. Now that the turn of the winter has passed, use a little fertilizer on any house plants which have begun to show new growth. Don't try to force these before they start.

Watch out for these pests inside: Red spider, aphids, white fly, mealy bug and scale. For aphids and mealy bug, use thick soapsuds and rinse off after an hour, or wipe off with a soft cloth dipped in soapsuds.

Scale must be scraped off by hand with cloth or brush and the foliage rinsed off later. Red spider is very difficult to get rid of and very easy to acquire. Remember that it cannot live in moist, cool, conditions and that the underside of the leaf is especially affected. Wash the leaves often with water as a preventive and keep the air moist and cool. White fly sucks the plant juices. There are sprays for some of these pests so investigate a good, all-around spray.

I speak from experience regarding that hateful red spider. A friend gave me a huge mother-in-law's-tongue and I was so delighted because I could get two or three out of that big plant. I found that it was simply full of red spiders so I sprayed and sprayed. I finally cut the whole thing back to about an inch or two and then knocked off the dirt from the roots and made two new big pots. Hopefully I am rid of red spiders.

Get all your trimming and shaping of shrubbery done as soon as possible. Avoid pruning of the trees which bleed, such as elms, maples, etc. This work is best done after the foliage is well developed, or left until September. Don't forget to be careful to trim only the flowering shrubs which bloom late in the season so you won't destroy the blossoming wood on the early blooming variety.

Giving the evergreens a dormant spray will help keep down the red spider as well as scale and other pests.

Now is the time to prune fruit trees. Good fruit is the result of careful pruning and spraying and all this activity must be done before the sap begins to rise.

Going Through the Garden

February 2 is Groundhog Day and let's hope he doesn't dive back underground and give us another six weeks of cold weather. I don't know about you but I have had my fill of cold weather. The only pleasure I get from this cold weather is knowing that any snakes in my yard are underground for a while, at least! I hope they came out too early and froze to death!

Birds are so much a part of a good garden that the coming of the first Robin in late February or March gladdens our hearts as few other sights can. It's just a notice that spring is on the way. Almost everyone wants birds in the garden but few know how to attract them. How wonderful it is to sit in a large garden of perennials, blooming shrubs and trees and watch birds all around. It certainly makes a garden a thing of beauty. And besides they are great workers.

Their chief needs are food and fresh water. During early spring freezes, the need for water becomes so acute that you can see them circling overhead looking for water. A pan of warm water in their accustomed watering place will solve this problem. We oftentimes let water in those ornamental bird baths become stagnant and worthless or even dangerous for the birds. Did you ever notice them around an automatic sprinkler on a hot summer day? Now you know how important fresh water is to birds. My spouse, who does not garden but is in charge of the birdbaths, keeps an old brush under the bath for scrubbing it out every time he fills it. Food consisting of a piece of suet wired to a tree limb, combined with seeds will keep them coming back year after year if they are supplied with water and suitable nesting places.

A little story that might interest you concerns my mother who moved into a small apartment when she was very old. She had a tiny patio which she could see from her chair. I planted two very fine roses beside the patio and kept them fed and watered along with a large flower box. Mama was very fond of birds and would scatter seeds on the patio so she could watch them eat. She also kept a bird bath full of water. From her I learned that if the bird bath is too deep, you must put a brick in it so they can stand or lie in the water. She called me one day to come at once and see something interesting. A mother Robin who had been eating on her patio had brought her brood of babies who could barely fly and they were all gathered on the patio. What pleasure she got from her roses and birds.

March is such a busy, busy time for gardeners that it's a good idea to do a few things now. Stock up on mulch. You may even find some leftover mulch at a bargain. You should wait till June, at least, to mulch but it's a good idea to have it ready. I have become very impressed with cypress mulch but there are other very good mulches. I like cypress mainly because there are no bugs in cypress for the nasty little garter snakes to hunt. It's most disconcerting to take a fork full of mulch only to find a snake hanging from the tines.

My grandmother had wonderful ways with roses. She had several of the old fashioned roses. She had some roses in rows but my memory doesn't tell me what they looked like on the bush, only what an individual rose looked like. When Pa cleaned out the stalls at the barn, he hauled some of that straw and manure to Ma's "back garden" for her mulch/fertilizer. That was always in spring. When she cleaned out the chicken houses, that also went to her flowers. Every year, when he cleaned out the tobacco barn, he hauled some of the old stalks to her garden. She crisscrossed those stalks around roses and lo and behold, she had systemic insecticide and some nitrogen to boot. The older I get, the smarter Ma gets. I often wonder how she managed to do so many things. She always had a cow to milk and chickens to feed, eggs to gather, nests to keep clean and in spring and summer, she had many baby chickens to tend. She also canned, preserved and dried everything possible. She was an immaculate housekeeper yet she managed time for quilting and best of all, she always had time to sit in the old porch swing with a little girl, whichever of the three granddaughters was there, and talk. And that, dear readers, is most important of all.

❀   ❀   ❀   ❀

There are a few necessary tools you need if you want to grow really beautiful roses and what gardener doesn't? Although you should try to use insect sprays as little as possible, you still will need a good insect spray for roses and a sprayer. Many gardeners like to use a combination insecticide and fungicide. The label will specify that it's a spray for diseases and insects. Though there are many good sprays, this is my preference and I keep a sprayer always ready. A good size for most of us rose fanciers is the one and a half gallon sprayer. It's light to carry and will spray a sizable number of roses. It's a good idea, while spraying roses, to look through your perennials for any plant that's being damaged by insects and/or mildew. It's best to use as little spray as possible but there comes a time when you must spray. The worst thing you can do in a flower garden is to spray everything, indiscriminately, killing good insects along with the bad.

You need a pair of good pruners for roses and perennials but the most useful tool in my arsenal is a pair of sewing scissors. Anytime you go into a flower bed, tuck those old scissors in your pocket along with a plastic bag. Some gardeners drop the deadheaded blooms and any other trash on the beds but most of us like to keep things a little neater. That's where the plastic bag comes in. One little word of caution: do NOT drop those scissors on the lawn. They play havoc with a lawn mower.

When cutting roses for the house, always remember to cut about an inch above a leaf bud which points outward. When deadheading spent blooms, cut in the same way. If you want to use the rose petals for potpourri, carry another bag. Soon you will look like a bag lady.

A really wonderful fertilizer to use when planting new annuals or perennials is a slow release fertilizer in granular form. It comes in a jar and will work up to 9 months. You just put a small amount, per directions, in the planting hole. Wonderful for us lazy gardeners. Occasionally, when I have a perennial which is not performing well, I dig it up carefully, put some of the granules in the hole and put the plant back in, water well and watch the improvement.

The "suckers" around roses come up around grafted roses and many times the grafted tea rose has frozen back and died, leaving only the old wild rose that was used for root in grafting. Many novice rose growers hate to cut down that healthy looking cane but it's a worthless thing so cut away.

Have you ever thought of growing roses in pots? There are some real advantages. The big advantage is that you can move them to follow the sun or to brighten a spot for a short time. The trick is to wrap the pot in layers of newspaper, then layers of brown paper and finally, wrap the whole pot in burlap. This works also with all the lilies and with daylilies. You want to mulch around them at least three inches to keep them cool. You could use green burlap to make them more attractive.

If you have wondered when to apply pre-emergent crabgrass killer to your lawn, the time is sometime in late February or early March. Believe it or not, the best way to do this at the right time is to watch your forsythia bush and when it blooms, it is the right time to apply crabgrass killer. If you wait until the crabgrass comes up, it's too late and you are wasting your time. Once you have applied it the first time, you apply it again in May. Now, if this is all just too much trouble, you could just learn to live with the hated crabgrass.

Do you have some perennials you wish you had moved last fall? Well, you can do this in very early spring. I would say, just as soon as you can work outside. Dig a hole with plenty of room for the plant, put some compost and/or dried manure in the bottom of the hole, water well and put the plant in and water again. Be sure to mulch well to keep in the moisture. Remember to tamp the soil down with your fist, never with your foot for fear of tearing the tender roots. This tamping of the soil is so important to keep from having air pockets, the sure killer in transplanting.

A tip to pass on to you is to plant a garlic clove beside each rose you plant to kill or repel (I don't know which) aphids. It's like a systemic insecticide much as Ma's tobacco stalks.

A message to rose growers who have asked for advice regarding the damage to their roses with the quick changes of weather: don't trim the damage yet.

Leave the dead stems until mid-February. There's an old gardener's date of St. Patrick's Day for the final trimming of roses. By that time, you can tell just where the dead stems are and give a final topping to the plant. Remember to always cut back to a live stem just above a leaf bud which faces outward. That keeps the center of the plant from getting crowded with leaves which causes mildew.

As soon as the daylilies start coming through the ground, I begin to think that maybe I haven't enough and also I should see about the newest colors. They are the easiest of all perennials to grow. Their needs are few. They need about an inch of water per week which means that you rarely have to water them except in the hot dry months of summer. There is such a variety of heights that you can find one for any spot in the garden. The most popular colors now are pinks, reds, purples and the ones which are almost white. If you want some in the back part of a garden, for distance viewing, the best colors are the golds and yellows. I prefer a lemon yellow for a splash of color and I have one which is of medium height with blooms so large that everyone thinks it's an oriental lily.

Landscapers love the Stella d'oro because of its small size and also it's perpetual blooming habit. They will be without blooms for very short intervals all summer. Now there are the minis with same habits and in a range of unbelievable colors. The thing I like best about the smaller daylilies is that you can move them around to spots that are bare, especially in borders.

One of the daylily's best qualities is that you can move them most anytime. I find it easier to cut them in half and move them in early spring but any old time seems to suit them. Just remember that they like sun best and don't like to be very dry.

Recently, I saw someone digging up something along the roadside and it dawned on me that that's where there are so many wild daylilies. I thought, to myself, "Oh, don't! You will be sorry."

They grow at unbelievable speed. It's said that they will grow a foot or more in all directions in a season and getting rid of them is not easy. In the first place, they bloom only once for a short time and with their habit of invasiveness, they are really not desirable. Keep in mind that the wild daylily, though a very distant ancestor of today's daylily, has almost none of its qualities. But please try to increase your daylily colors this year.

Since late winter or early spring, whichever you choose to call it, pruning of roses is of concern to most rose growers, this is a subject which needs some more clarification.

It's important to do your pruning with high-quality pruning shears. To keep from spreading disease from one rose to another, wipe the shears with alcohol after pruning each rose. It seems a lot of trouble but well worth it if you think of spreading disease all over your rose bed.

After pruning, paint each stem with Elmer's wood glue or nail polish to keep cane borers from attacking the newly cut canes.

All this is best done as early as you can tell where the new growth stops. The rest of your pruning depends on whether your roses bloom on new growth or old. Those that bloom on new growth are the Hybrid Tea roses, Grandifloras, Miniatures, Floribundas and the China roses. These need really hard pruning. While you are pruning out dead stems, cut out any cross branches or those stems which grow toward the inside. That's to keep air circulating. Remember you want to prune so that the stems are shaped like a vase with the inside of the plant free of stems.

On Miniature roses, cut back some of the oldest canes all the way to the base and shape the remaining stems by cutting back at least a third all over. Pruning climbing roses is done in two ways. On those that repeat blooming, prune them in late winter during their dormancy. Those that bloom only once need to be pruned after they bloom. On climbers, trim the side stems several inches in late winter and remove one or two of the oldest canes all the way to the ground.

On grafted roses, watch for "suckers," those stems that come up from the roots, and remove them all the way to the root. They will never bloom and take food from the rest of the plant.

Watering and fertilizing are the secret to beautiful roses. We know that good soil is a given so not mentioned here. Healthy roses need little spraying for insects and disease and as little as possible then.

Deadheading is probably one of the most neglected things we do for our roses and one of the most important. The best pruning and deadheading is done by cutting for use in the house. Always remember to cut about ¼ inch above a leaf bud pointing outwards. If you are just going through your beds deadheading, cut back the same way.

If fertilizing with the liquid method, the one applied with a jug on the end of the hose, is more work than you are prepared to do, think about using a slow-release fertilizer this year. Just a small amount under the new plant, while you are planting, will last for up to nine months and sure is better than dragging the hose around. It's just another work saver for the lazy gardener.

Some gardening chores can be put off till "later" and some have to be done at just the right time of the season. About the first of March or even late February, Chrysanthemums will start coming up. Then is the time to dig and separate them into smaller clumps. Plant them about 18 inches to 2 feet apart. Always remember that Chrysanthemums need full sun. When they are about 5 inches high, start pinching them back. That means to pinch about an inch from every single little branch. You will need to repeat this procedure every two or three weeks until early July. This keeps them short and stocky and full for fall blooms. If you water them thoroughly when you move them, they won't notice they've been moved. I like to plant them in some out of the way place because when fall comes and they start budding, it's time to move them into a prominent place in the front garden.

Another time that must be just right is the timing for fertilizing spring bulbs. When they are just coming through the soil, give them some fertilizer, 10-10-10 or bulb fertilizer. That will keep you watching carefully because they just seem to grow inches overnight once they start.

Be very careful in weeding when the weather starts getting warm because many of the self-sowing plants will have little seedlings coming up.

As you may know, the bulb commonly known as the jonquil and also the bulb with the clusters of sweet smelling flowers are both narcissi, the plural of narcissus. The buttercup is also the same. I tell you this so you won't be embarrassed by using the incorrect term in the company of the "knowledgeable" gardeners. As if you cared!

Jonquils always remind me of Ma's old garden. Lewis women had been planting and tending bulbs for more than a hundred years in that big old yard. She had clumps of them everywhere. By the time I was old enough to pick them, I pretty much kept the blooms all picked. She had vases of them everywhere and never a cross word to me. I never heard her say, "Don't pick the flowers."

My very favorite time of the year is when the perennials start coming up. I often forget what is planted where (forgetting to mark them) and I always get many surprises. If you want to break up a big clump of perennials, this early time is right for transplanting a part of a clump. You often can get two or three starters from a big clump. Always water when moving anything.

There is nothing like compost for those perennial beds. Just sprinkle some all over the bed and then give the whole bed a little aerating by poking holes with your fork.

This is also a great time to separate daylilies. I always try to remember that the old daylily leaves, which I didn't get cut down, is a place for the early critters like the garter snakes. The beauty of day lilies is that you can hardly hurt them, no matter what you do to them. I always like to advise any gardener to pick up at least one new day lily when taking those early strolls through the nurseries. Later in the spring there's little time to go through the whole nursery. I always feel that the day lily is the backbone of my flower beds. At least until the tall garden phlox starts blooming. The new colors of the day lilies each year seem to get better and better.

If you are an iris fancier, be sure to pick up all dead iris leaves and burn them. They harbor the dreaded iris borer and lie dormant in the leaves. They can move over a wide area of your iris bed in a short time once they get into the fresh new plant.

A most important chore in early spring is to stake your perennials just as they are high enough to identify. Once they start growing, it's too late to do a good job. You know the ones that need staking. They are the ones that fall over about the time they are at their best. When peonies are in full bloom, it seems that's the time we have the big rain storm and you look out to find the whole plant sagging to the ground. Staking them early prevents this catastrophe.

Most gardeners worry about a cold spell coming when the roses have begun to put out leaf buds and when the perennials start coming up. Don't worry. They can stand more cold than you think. The leaf buds will just turn black and drop off, to be replaced by more leaf buds. Mother Nature seems to have things in hand. The few that a freeze will upset are bulbs which have already put up flower buds and peonies starting to bud. It won't kill them though, just affects the flowers for this spring.

Remember the old saying that a gardener needs a strong back with a hinge in the middle.

MARCH

Oh, boy! It's March and things will finally start happening. We can finally get out and play in the dirt. The bulbs are flowering into bright yellows, the basketball season is winding down and the lawn is getting ready for hot weather. And isn't it grand!

There are many things that you can do in March and here are some of them. You can sow grass seeds in bare spots. Though spring is not the best time, it beats nothing. As soon as the temperatures start hitting the low 60's, you can sow. Just don't waste those seeds and your time if we have a cold March.

Using a high-nitrogen fertilizer, you can also fertilize your lawn this month but be sure to just lightly fertilize. Too much fertilizer gives too much fast growth, weakening the root system. Most of the weeds

37

haven't come up yet so you may waste money on weed and feed. I would rather get at the weeds later with a liquid spray, the ones that attach to the hose. It's fast and sure.

When mowing in March or April, remember to keep the mower at 2 inches or 2½. Better to mow often in spring than to mow with the mower set too low. You can throw the root system into shock. Also it encourages disease and bugs.

If you are thinking of employing a lawn care service, be very careful in selecting one. My brother-in-law came home one day to find a young boy from his lawn care service. He smelled a familiar odor and knew at once it was not the right chemical. It was a grass and weed killer. Most of his lawn and some of his roses had been sprayed. With a lot of washing with hoses, they were able to save most of the roses and some of the grass. Just a word of warning that some of those lawn care people are more reputable than others.

If you want to transplant or divide some perennials, do it when the soil is dry enough to be easily handled. Never transplant when the soil is wet. The plants that are most successfully transplanted in early spring are the ones that bloomed in fall. All perennials do best from vigorous new plants. DO NOT try to move or divide Peonies in spring.

Someone is always asking me about Sweet Peas. It seems there's little written about this old favorite which is coming back in popularity. They are best planted at the traditional time of March 17th. Don't ask me why. It's just one of those dates set in stone. They require a rich, deeply worked soil which contains some clay. Open sunny locations are best. Some gardeners dig a deep trench in fall in preparation for early planting in spring. They cover the trench with leaves till spring. But since you didn't do that, dig trenches about 2 feet deep and the width of a spade. Fill the trench with good topsoil and manure, well mixed, and sow the seeds about two inches below the surface. The young plants can be hilled up occasionally as they grow. The seedlings have to be thinned to about six inches apart when they begin to grow. I hope you consider some Sweet Peas if you have the space. The flowers must be kept closely picked as the vine dies as soon as seed pods form. This plant is a deep rooter and will not thrive unless they have this deep cultivation such as the trench above. Feed every four weeks or so with a fertilizer designed for blooming perennials which will be low in nitrogen and high in phosphorous and potash. Because of its deep roots, it will be necessary to water well. I always think of my Ma when I see Sweet Peas. She loved to use them in great bunches as cut flowers.

At this time of year, many of the spring blooming plants may be forced by bringing them indoors in clumps. Water them well, have good drainage and remember to keep them cool at first so they can acclimate themselves to indoors. Select a day when the ground is frozen but not hard enough to prevent you from digging out clumps of Dwarf Iris, Violets, Crocus, Scillas and a few other bulbs in bowls or pots. I have an abundance of Dwarf Iris and have given them to anyone who would take them. Now, this is a good way to dig up some more. They just seem to thrive anywhere I put them.

All gardeners that I know wish for an early spring so we can get out and wear ourselves down and break our backs, digging and planting. Sometimes we just have to "sit on it" until warmer weather, but a few of the cool-season flowers can be planted in March. Some of these are snapdragons, pansies, sweet williams and a few others. When you see these plants in the displays, take them home and plant them. It's OK. They are very tough. In fact, they will keep right on blooming after a light frost. They can be put out from mid March on through April. Nothing gladdens the heart of a gardener as those lovely sweet williams in early spring. My grandmother called them pinks and that's what they are to me.

After your spring-flowering bulbs have faded, cut off the spent flower stalks and feed the plants with 5-10-5 fertilizer, about ½ cup per 10 square feet of beds. If you fed them as they were emerging this spring, forget this step. Do not remove the foliage after the flower fades. They must stay alive until they begin to yellow to feed the bulb underneath. A gardener of dubious gardening know-how told me recently that he just mowed them down. Of course, his flowers will be smaller and smaller and fewer and fewer.

MARCH

One question I'm asked every spring is, "When can I transplant and divide my Hostas?" And the answer is to do it now. The earlier, the better. Just be sure the soil is dry enough to work easily. Those Hostas sure can jazz up a shady corner. The newer ones come in such a variety of sizes and colors. Some shrubs which will grow in that shady place you have are the glossy abelia, grape holly or witch hazel. And for trees in shady spots, try the dogwood, redbud and Canadian hemlock. The grape holly will have a tag calling it Oregon grape holly. It's a really attractive shrub, especially after the "grapes" form. So don't give up on shady spots.

March is a good time to bathe houseplants to get them ready to put outside when the weather gets really warm. This could be the last part of March but with a cold spring, it could be mid-April. To bathe houseplants, first fill a tub or sink with warm water and add a flake soap such as Ivory Flakes. Put the pot in a plastic bag, tie the top so that dirt doesn't get wet and fill your tub or the sink. Turn the pot upside down and swish the leaves in the water. This will get rid of all the winter's grime and spider mites, if you think you have some. Houseplants can use this bath several times a year but don't try this on the fuzzy leafed varieties such as your African violets. Also don't do this to ferns and the succulents.

It's also time to start feeding your indoor plants about every two weeks to get them ready to move outside. There are some good water-soluble fertilizers that are 18-18-18 or 20-20-20.

41

If you saved caladium tubers from last year, or if you have to buy some from a garden center, start them indoors now for those wonderfully showy leaves next summer. Plant the tubers about an inch deep in flats or in individual small pots and keep them in bright sunlight. When the outside temperature gets up to 60 degrees, you can move them outside.

One thing the successful gardener must learn is to know when to be in a hurry and when to restrain himself or herself. With the first warm days of March, or even the last of February, it is a temptation to get out there and remove all the winter mulch and un-cover any plants which you have covered for the winter. It's been said that when you get that impulse, take a trip for a couple of weeks and start all that uncovering when you get back. There are so many other things to do that your energy is better spent at other things. It is a good thing to loosen mulch with a fork in early spring to let the mulch dry out and let air penetrate. It's usually April before you should re-move the larger pieces of covering and moving the mulch around to cultivate some plants.

If you have thought about sowing some grass seeds, a good time is about the middle of March. That gives the seeds about a month of rains which they must have. If you wait till warm weather, just forget about sowing till fall. And be sure to buy seeds guar-anteed to be at least 98% free of weeds. As in most things, the better seeds are more expensive but who wants to sow weed seeds?

Many new gardeners want to know more about the beautiful clematis. There are so many new colors and varieties but my favorite is still the Jackmani with the strong color. The question some gardeners have is to prune or not to prune. First, the soil must be rich, well-drained and slightly acid. They thrive in peaty soil if it's limed thoroughly; peat alone is too acid. They must have shaded roots and partial shade is all right for the vine. They need a very thick mulch for winter. I like to plant a couple of hostas next to the root to provide that shade. I have also seen a box, 8 or 10 inches tall, all around to provide shade. The reason for the shade is that clematis roots are very shallow and need protection from the sun. As you might guess, cultivation must be shallow, if at all. As for pruning, the varieties which first bloom in July, and Jackmani is one of those, can be pruned to within 2 feet of the ground in March. That will stimulate new growth. If you have new plants, I would wait a year or two to prune. Many gardeners only prune out the oldest vines which have become weakened. As to pruning the varieties which bloom first in spring and again in fall, to preserve both blooming seasons, little pruning must be done. You can always prune out any dead stems and you will soon know which are putting out little leaf buds.

A favorite of all the blooming shrubs is about to make a debut, the beautiful azaleas. Azaleas should be carefully planted and here are some tips you might like to know. First, their roots are shallow but wide. So, when digging a hole, you need a wide, shallow hole to encourage roots to grow out, not down. They need rich soil. They also need to grow in dappled shade though some growers brag that they grow azaleas in full sun. I haven't seen them do well in sun though. As you already know, they love acid soil so be sure to buy special fertilizer for acid loving plants. Each year, you should prune out the biggest branch to encourage shoots to come up inside the plant to make a full shrub. Other than that one big branch to prune, you can do a little pruning throughout the year just to keep a nice shape.

When buying fertilizer, keep in mind that the three numbers on the bag are very important. The middle number should be high for flowers and the first number is nitrogen and you don't want high nitrogen for anything in your yard that blooms, including perennials, annuals and blooming shrubs. The best advice for any gardener is to buy from a good nursery and ask questions. If the first person seems to be too busy, ask for the manager. I guarantee the manager won't be too busy for you. When I go to a nursery and want an answer for a special question, I find it very disconcerting to find that the only person available is some teenager too young to know.

Remember when you're planning a flower bed that the closer you plant perennials (or annuals), the less soil will show and the fewer weeds you will have.

Another tip: don't start digging around in the beds just yet. Some little seedlings may start coming up when the soil warms up. I am always nervous waiting to see if my necotiana seedlings will come up. I enjoy all the free plants that I get from seedlings.

Another little surprise that I am expecting to see soon is the nasty little garter snake. They are early risers from hibernation and like to sun on my rocks. I now have a new weapon, I'm feeding some big Tom cat near the rocks and I hope he is a snake killer. Some neighbor is probably wondering why their cat isn't hungry.

APRIL

To dethatch or not to dethatch, that is the question. We talk a lot about it but most of us do little about it. In reality, most of us don't need to dethatch. Unless you have from ½ to 1 inch of thatch, we don't need to do anything. Thatch is layers of organic matter that develop from too much fertilizing and watering. Tall fescue and ryegrass don't develop thatch to amount to anything. If you find that there is enough thatch in your lawn to interfere with water and air getting to the roots, then dethatch you must. You can rent a dethatcher at most lawn and garden stores. It cuts down to the soil and brings the whole mess to the top of the grass. You may need to crisscross your lawn a few times to get all the thatch. The organic matter is easily raked up and what a great addition to your compost pile! Too much watering can be bad for your lawn as well as not enough watering. You may want to measure your sprinkler system. Just remember that the temperamental Bluegrass is less-drought-tolerant and a Bluegrass lawn may need more dethatching.

It's a sobering thought but there are some of us gardeners who just can't seem to grow certain perennials. Some will look good for a season or two and just disappear. This gardener is no exception. Some have trouble with delphiniums and foxglove. And then some have trouble with other plants. The best advice is to read the tag which comes with each plant and plant accordingly. Use all the information you can get from the Web, from books and from other gardeners. Many times, the answer is as simple as over or under watering. Other times, it's lack of some little piece of information. I'm sometimes reminded of the years I tried to grow Oriental Poppies. Each time, they just died down and I dug up the dead roots and replanted with something else. Slow to learn was I! They naturally die back after blooming and then revive in late summer. That little bit of information had escaped me somehow.

Another tip when planting trees which came bare-rooted from a catalog is to soak those roots in a bucket of cool water for at least 24 hours. The same advice goes for any shrubs which come without soil.

If you have a small garden and want to grow some of the early crops such as broccoli, cabbage and cauliflower, remember that April can have some very

cold days and those baby plants may need some protection. A gallon-sized plastic milk jug is just the
thing. It keeps out rabbits and birds and can provide
a cover from frost. The broccoli and cauliflower,
though they are early crops, can't cope with very cold
weather. When I first moved to Minnesota, I made a
friend of a great gardener. One early spring day, I
found him covering everything in his garden with
milk jugs with the bottoms cut out and their caps still
screwed on. Funniest looking garden I ever saw but I
was soon accustomed to this sight in gardens everywhere. This same good gardener came to our house
and heavily fertilized my black-eyed peas and limas,
plants which he knew nothing about. The soil, being
already too rich for either plant, just went wild. You
never saw such vines and no peas. Same with the
limas. Lesson here is that none of us knows everything! I did, however, learn to really use those milk
jugs. I learned to blanch cauliflower heads by placing the leaves over the heads and then tying up the
whole thing. Later I learned that you can blanch cauliflower heads by tucking a piece of aluminum foil
inside the leaves.

April is a good time to fertilize evergreens which
usually need an acid-type fertilizer. The exception is
the yew or taxus and that evergreen needs a 10-10-10
fertilizer. Did you know that you shouldn't plant a
yew near rhododendrons or azaleas because they love
acid and the yew won't tolerate it?

Sometimes I want to stop and tell a homeowner
not to do something which I know is a mistake. One

such temptation regards shallow rooted plants which I see with way too much mulch. Those plants are azaleas, rhododendrons, boxwoods, dogwoods and a few others. If you keep adding mulch every year, it "suffocates" the plant. This also leads to diseases. I sometimes see up to a foot of mulch when only two or three inches is enough. You may as well take a spray and kill them off. Even though I know it looks good, it's bad. If you want to see that fresh, black look of mulch, take off all the old and add 2 or 3 inches of fresh mulch.

If you are lucky enough to get a lily for Easter, some basic rules of care are as follows: They need bright sun, the soil should be kept slightly damp but not soggy wet, and they need to have a hole in the bottom of that fancy foil cover. After the flowers fade, set the plant outside in the sun. In a week or so, remove the plant from the pot and plant it in a sunny spot in rich soil. It will make a beautiful addition to your garden and bloom and multiply for years.

Although the average frost date for most of Kentucky is in the early part of April, it's always possible to have a frost during this month of uncertainty, so it's still too soon to set out those more sensitive plants. I always set out a few snapdragons throughout my flower beds to fill in spaces with color and because I like them. I have them all ready to set out if it ever warms up. Then, later on, Necotiana seedlings will come up from seeds dropped from last year's plant. Those two make great additions to a perennial bed. The date for setting out those sensitive annuals is May 15. Don't ask me why or how that date was set. It works out pretty well, though.

After a cold winter, you may find some damage to magnolias. The leaves may look brown but never fear. Fertilize them with a special formula for magnolias and water them this summer during dry spells and all will be well with your magnolia.

You may also notice that some of your evergreens are brown at the tips. This is also from having the ground frozen during a prolonged cold spell.

One more time: spray your evergreens in April to prevent bagworms. Once you see the "bags", you're in trouble.

Evergreens in need of shaping and thickening may be sheared in April as the new growth gets under way. This is also a good time to shape boxwood.

Trees and shrubs that prefer spring planting are birches, magnolias, tulip trees, Japanese maples, altheas, flowering almonds, ornamental cherries, buddleias (butterfly bush), rhododendrons and weigelas.

Pinch back asters, dahlias, cosmos, zinnias, salvias and chrysanthemums after they are a few inches high. Pinch off the growing tips between thumb and forefinger to encourage side shoots and bushier plants. Continue pinching mums every two weeks or so until the first week in July. Then let them start flower buds for fall blooms.

To win the battle of the weeds, weed regularly and thoroughly. The best time is just after a rain when the whole root system comes up. Many of the newer daylilies need to be divided about every 3 to 4 years. If you plan to dig up a whole clump, wait till after the first bloom. But to divide a clump in two sections, place a sharp spade in the middle of the plant and separate the whole section to replant somewhere else or give to a gardener friend. That kind of division can be done any time. They just don't seem to care.

After daffodils have bloomed, cut back the dead flower stalk. Never tie or rubber band the leaves. They may be ugly as they ripen but tying or braiding them lowers the plant vitality. Also, once the leaves have yellowed and fallen over, it's better to cut them off rather than pull them off. Pulling them leaves a hole, which may let a nasty little narcissus fly in.

If you're thinking of a climbing rose and aren't an experienced rose grower, consider the old favorite climber Blaze. It's extremely impervious to Japanese Beetles and blackspot. Also it blooms profusely all season long. Since it's a very old rose, it's very inexpensive. What more can you ask of a climber?

This is a good time to dig up and replant rooted suckers from shrubs. It may take a long time for them to mature but sooner or later, they will.

In April and early May, when tulips are at their best, don't you regret that you didn't plant more bulbs last fall? By careful planning, you can have splashes of color from bulbs lasting through the final tulip blooms in late May to the glads and dahlias at the end of the season. However the spring show put on by hyacinths, daffodils and tulips is most pleasing.

There are some very important considerations when planning bulbs for spring blooms. First, make a rough scale drawing of your beds where you want bulbs. Remember that the most important thing is good drainage. A general rule of thumb is to plant bulbs about three times deeper than the length of the bulb. You can use an auger to drill holes or you can use a bulb planter which soon wears your hand out. Or, like me, you can put the shovel down to the depth you want, rock it back and forth a bit and stick the bulb down beside the shovel. Watering after planting bulbs will start new root growth at once. Remember, I'm not a frugal gardener but I am a lazy one. As an old Norwegian in Northern Minnesota once told me, "If you don't use your head, then you must use your feet!"

Spring-flowering bulbs should be planted in October to get root growth before winter. Be careful in buying bulbs. You want large, firm bulbs without any blemishes. Now, if you can't plant in October, they can be planted as late as January as long as you can work the soil.

At Churchill Downs, where they have the beautiful tulip beds, they plant after the racing season which is usually after Thanksgiving. Would you believe that they do not save last year's bulbs? They buy all new bulbs. That has always boggled my mind. Many gardeners don't like the unsightly yellowing tops of bulbs. There's a little trick that I have used. When the foliage of tulips begin to yellow, dig them up and put them in a trench in some out of the way place where they won't be seen as they ripen. Once the tops are shriveled, take the bulbs out and lay them in a sunny place to dry. Then store them in a dry basement or garden shed till planting time next fall. You will have bigger and better tulips. Don't do as I did once. I forgot that box full of bulbs until the following spring and had to throw them out. You can do the same routine with hyacinths and they will continue to be large blooms as when you first bought them.

If you want to move some jonquils either because they are crowded and don't bloom well or because the blooms are getting smaller and smaller, wait until the tops have fully ripened and yellowed. Then you can dig and separate them and plant them where you want them.

The jonquils (daffodils or narcissi) are by far the easiest the easiest grown of all bulb types, being free from disease and trouble. Someone has said: "All you do is plant them, cover them and forget them until they remind you by blooming in the spring." No hoeing, no weeding, no pruning.

It's important to buy number one bulbs from a reliable dealer. Beware of some catalog with big bargains. You need not go to the extreme for the largest bulb. Did you know that voles won't even eat them?

Remember that the touch of fresh manure means certain death to bulbs. More failures come from fresh manure than any other cause. If you want to use manure for a bed in fall, mix it with the soil in the bed, turn it several times in summer and carefully mix it in fall before planting bulbs. The ideal bed is made up of a top foot of a rich sandy loam free of stagnant water but will hold moisture.

If you absolutely must move bulbs before they ripen, lift them with a big clump of soil and, above all, get them in the ground immediately.

Of the several kinds of iris, all of which are worth cultivating, tall bearded varieties lead all the rest in well deserved popularity. Those are the ones you grew up picking in Grandma's garden. I loved Ma's iris and I can still remember the perfume of a vase full of her old iris on the dining room table. Once, they all were purple and there were groups of them in every yard. Now, there are so many colors and shades as to boggle the mind. Also some now bloom twice each summer. For ease of culture and for the ability to stand neglect, they are unsurpassed.

They need little attention but because they are strong growers, they need to be divided every two to five years if you want the best blooms. Left longer, they fill the bed and choke themselves to death.

The time to divide is soon after they finish blooming so they will become established before next spring. Most growers agree that the best method of dividing this Iris is to transplant only a part of a bed each year. This allows for a succession of strong plants and sturdy blooms.

Transplanting iris can become so complicated as to fill a whole book, but the gist is to remove all the old, weak roots since they are of no value and most gardeners leave at least three roots in a clump. After transplanting, the leaves should be cut back to relieve stress on the root structure. Some growers do that each spring because it seems to look better but is very unwise because it affects the blooms the following year.

The rhizomes do not need rich soil, will not tolerate manure, and thrive on hillsides and raised beds or on banks. Full sun is best but partial shade might be tolerated. They grow well in clay soil if a little sand has been added. Someone has said that if a soil will grow corn, it will grow Iris. In digging a bed, work in deeply some manure so well rotted as to not look like manure along with a little lime and sand. Literally pulverize this soil before planting. Use no chemical fertilizer and do not mulch. A little wood ashes work well and some growers use some bone meal.

Bearded iris have few enemies, the only common one being root rot and the iris borer. The borer lays eggs in the leaves and after they hatch at flowering time, enter the rhizome or root and kill your whole bed. If you look through the bed, you may find some mushy looking plants which must be dug and destroyed. In spring, the eggs are just below the dead leaves and (you aren't going to believe this) some growers destroy them by fire. They sprinkle the dead leaves with a tiny bit of gasoline. Don't allow a prolonged fire to injure the plant. This is not for me but you may have heard of this practice.

There are several other varieties of iris. The Siberian iris likes gritty damp soil. English, Spanish, Dutch Iris like well-drained loose soil. The Dwarf Iris is a rock garden plant and is absolutely beautiful in early to mid-April. In fact, I have the Dwarf Iris in deep purple, snow white, deep yellow, light yellow and deep wine. They are such prolific little things that I have given many away. This little plant wants thorough drainage and doesn't care if they are dry all summer. I keep them at the edge of my flower beds as an edging or along with other plants among some rocks. I also have Siberian iris which I find very attractive though they require a lot of watering.

Some other popular varieties of spring flowering bulbs are so well known and are so well described in catalogs, that I won't describe them but will give you names of a few. The best known are crocus, glory in the snow, snowdrops (who can forget those blooming in old gardens?), spring snowflakes, grape hyacinths, scillas and star of Bethlehem. All are desirable except for the last one, the star of Bethlehem. It's not very pretty and is the worst little pest you will ever have. Since I admit to trying to reduce all the work I can in my flower beds, I like best those bulbs which are easiest to grow and which require little of me. The head of the class is undoubtedly the narcissi. They have just about all the most desirable attributes. I have some which came from Ma's old yard. Some are the old trumpet shaped yellow daffodils and another is the little flat cluster of wonderfully fragrant blooms which Ma called narcissus. These I have moved with me any time we change locations. Over the years, I have added many others including one snow white large daffodil and others which are double or with red centers or variegated.

But all of the spring flowering bulbs are welcome after a long cold winter.

MAY

We hope you have your tools ready and on hand to keep up the appearance of your garden during the summer. May is the month when eleven months of effort come to fruition and everything looks its best. But to keep it that way is another matter.

The importance of proper labeling is felt very often in spring. The areas in the perennial border in which the late maturing plants are placed are often dug up, ruining the plants we have forgotten. The Platycodons or Bell-flowers, Hosta, Bleedingheart and some of the tiny bulbs are easily killed by a little probing with a hoe or shovel. Permanent markers would avoid this loss. While you're at it, mark the other, older flowers in your beds while they are in flower and easily identified.

MAY

It's time to sow those tender annuals such as amaranth, petunia, torenia, gomphrena, portulaca and any other of the plants which are hurt by late cold spells. The date for planting in our area has always been May 15, another of those dates handed down from gardener to gardener.

You can sow gourd seeds in late May or early June in the sun and in light loam, enriched with very old manure. Ten seeds to the hill is recommended. Remember that gourds should be planted where you want them to grow since they don't transplant easily. Provide support while they are very small plants. I used my neighbor's fence (with permission, I think) and wound up with vines running twenty feet on each side of one hill. That wasn't so bad but picking off the dead, dried tendrils that fall was a very long job.

When you are transplanting those seedlings from flats into open ground, loosen carefully the rootlets which have made a tight wad so they can take up water and food. Dig the hole, fill it with water and place some Osmacote in the hole; then place the seedling in position and fill up with dry soil and water no more. There won't be any moisture on the surface of the soil for the sun to bake or steam. Keep the plants covered with a little newspaper or flower pots for a few days. Now they're off to a great start.

To insure a stocky growth of annuals, remove the central bud at the top of the plant when it's about six inches tall. Ageratum, calendulas, snapdragons, stocks, marigolds, alyssum and petunias are plants needing such treatment. poppies, asters, and nicotiana are best left alone.

Now you can see what you need in the way of replacement of perennials so off to the nurseries! Buy only hardy clumps and select a cool cloudy day for planting. Better to hold the plants for a day or two rather than plant on windy, sunny days.

Start planting gladiolus May 15 and plant every two weeks until July 10th to get blooms through September. I feel fortunate to have a few hardy glads. Some gardeners shy away from them because they are so gaudy but they make such a great splash in an otherwise dull border.

I am happy to relate that Miracle Grow has a new product which I am using. Instead of dragging the hoses around with the sprayer attached with the Miracle Grow powder, this year I am using their new pellet fertilizer. I hope to do away with a lot of summer work. I noticed that other companies also are selling this new form of fertilizer.

The best way to prune spirea, weigela, abelia, Japanese quince and climbing roses is to cut long sprays to give to friends, the church and the sick. Some other perennials and biennials will bloom longer if cut freely. Don't let seeds form. It's no wonder my grandmother had such beautiful flowers. She cut great bunches of everything in bloom for her house and to take to our little family graveyard and to neighbors on a summer afternoon of quilting and gossip. One very happy memory is of my dear grandmother and her bucket of water going from plant to plant, gathering flowers. We even cut the honeysuckle vine on the fence by the road. Anything that bloomed was beautiful to Ma.

In early May, you can plant glads. Plant them about 6 inches apart or plant them 12 inches apart and plant more in between every two weeks, giving you blooms all summer. Late June is the latest time to plant them. Plant about 4 to 6 inches deep and spade deeply because their roots are long. They need fertilizer just as any other flower in your perennial bed. I think they look best in the mixed beds planted in clusters, giving you color all summer.

Start staking taller perennials such as the tall phlox. They will grow in an upright position and look so much better if staked while small. Nearly all tall flowers benefit by staking. It's particularly true of larkspur, hollyhocks, foxgloves, dahlias and gladioli. Use strong stakes like bamboo or wooden ones and tie the plant to the stake in more than one place. As a tie, you can use raffia or coarse green cord especially for staking or you could use my old favorites cut from old nylon stockings.

Do you need to prune your conifers? If you want to prune for bushier, denser trees, prune off the "candles", those little light green tips of the limbs that stand upright. Cutting off old limbs won't produce more growth; they just look worse.

As soon as your peonies have bloomed, remove all old faded blooms to get more blooms next year. Don't try to move or divide them until next September or October. They go into shock if moved during the period when they're making blooms for next spring. It takes years for them to recover and bloom again. Have you ever wondered why there are ants on the peony buds? They eat the sweet, sticky stuff on the buds. The buds can't open with the sticky stuff on them. That's a theory and as good as any. Fertilize peonies all summer along with all other perennials. Mulch peonies very lightly if at all and keep all weeds and grass pulled from around the plants. If you haven't already done so, stake your peonies. There will surely come a really hard rain to ruin the looks of peonies if you fail to stake them.

When planting annuals, drop the whole section of little plants into a bucket of water for just a minute. The hardest part is pinching out the tops of annuals to make them fuller, especially ageratum, snapdragons, marigolds, annual phlox, alyssum and petunias. The exceptions are poppies, asters and nicotiana. The latter three are not happy to be pinched back.

Staking most annuals makes your flower beds look so much nicer. Even the smaller plants will stand upright and look better with a small stake. An old coat hanger, straightened and cut half, makes a good stake for smaller plants.

If you haven't already planted your tomatoes, try sinking a tin can (both ends cut out, of course) around the stems to keep cutworms from having a picnic on those tender plants. Those "Easter lilies" will last for years and years with just a little care. After the flower has faded, set the pot outside in full sun. After the lily has become acclimated, set the bulb in a sunny spot among other flowers. It might even bloom again this year. Not likely but possible. They multiply like rabbits once they are established. My Ma had an enormous bed of them in her back garden and I loved to cut them for a vase of mixed flowers. Ma believed that flowers should be cut by grandchildren anytime.

You have often heard that the sense of smell brings back more memories than any of the other senses. Anyone who has ever been anaesthetized with ether, and it's been a long time, can attest to that. Then there are other perfumes that bring wonderful people to mind. When I smell the aroma of Sweet William Pinks, I immediately think of my wonderful grandmother. She had two beds of them in a rock garden in front of the long front porch. They were the only flowers I couldn't pick. I finally understood that they self seed and they had been there for many, many years. They were planted by Pa's mother and were very important. When the flowers faded, Ma let some go to seed and then she would spread those seeds throughout the little rock garden beds. This great-grandmother of mine who had first planted them had been an avid gardener and had planted many "old-fashioned" roses which still grew along the garden fence and near the front porch. One beautiful red one was my grandfather's favorite because it triggered special memories of his adored mother. My mother loved lily-of-the-valley and even wore that perfume for many years so I associate that scent with her. Each year when they bloom, I remember the bottle of perfume on her dresser and that special aroma around her. Because Mother's Day is coming up, I want to remind those of you who have living mothers how very fortunate you are. Someday you probably will have a memory stored away of a special scent that brings back memories. I often wish that my dear Ma could know that I have shared my love for her with readers from all over the country. She would certainly be amazed.

If you are looking for a Mother's Day gift, it's not too late to buy potted roses. If planted carefully, they will do just fine. Another great gift would be some lily bulbs. Many bulbs of the showy lilies are for sale now. These are not daylilies but the big fancy lilies such as the Regal. They should be planted three times the height of the bulbs. That is, if the bulb is two inches high, its top should be four inches below the top of the soil. If you think on that for a minute, you'll see that's mathematically right.

May is the time when we just can't resist those hanging baskets of flowers in all the garden centers. But we tend to forget how much trouble they are. Also most of them can't stand direct sun and can only tolerate some filtered sun in the morning. That goes double for the fern. Those baskets probably will have to be watered daily and misted often. Also fuchsias draw white flies. Are you sure you still want a hanging basket? If you still want one, check to be sure that there is a drainage hole in the bottom.

It's time to set your mower blade to 2 ½ to 3 inches. And keep those blades sharp.

At the risk of becoming boring regarding the bag worm, I remind you that May is when the bag worms come out of the tiny bags on your evergreens. Search very carefully for the bags, even the tiny ones. If you find any evidence, a spraying with good old Orthene will do the job. It's remarkable how quickly they can destroy an evergreen.

The big leaf hydrangeas are putting up shoots and will be in bloom shortly. Don't cut out any old dead looking stems until you are sure no leaves will come out on them. Remember that you can determine their color by adding lime to make them pink or acid fertilizer to make them blue. They prefer light shade and rich moist soil so remember to water them often in summer. Early fall is the best time to plant these hydrangeas but if you are presented with one as a gift, by all means get it in your garden. If you decide to buy one, be sure to buy one in bloom and don't buy one with brown or wilted leaves. If one is not in bloom, leave it alone. Hydrangeas often have powdery mildew. If so, pick off the infected parts and spray with a fungicide which lists powdery mildew on the container. The lovely part of the big leaf hydrangeas is that the large flower clusters dry well for a nice winter bouquet. Simply pick them with long stems, tie them together and hang, upside down, somewhere in the house. Easy!

If you discover that the tops of your daylilies seem to have been eaten, look for a marauding rabbit. They seem to love the tender daylily tops in spring.

When planting dahlia tubers, drive the stake into the soil as you plant. If you try to stake them after they start growing, you can damage the tender roots.

You've heard, "You can't teach an old dog new tricks." Well, it's not so. You're never too old to learn. Recently, I admired a wisteria tree in Elizabeth Tinsley's yard so I called her to find out where she bought the "tree". I was very confused to find out that it was just a vine which had been trained to be a tree. She had started out with a small vine and as it grew, she shaped it into an umbrella-shaped tree. I imagine one would have to stake the trunk as it grew. She said that her tree had to be pruned every week or two to keep the vines from growing into a neighboring tree. I was so intrigued with the whole idea that I consulted my nursery friend, Steve, and learned more about the beautiful wisteria tree. He said that another problem is that eventually the trunk of the wisteria tree gets very large and that the whole thing has to be cut down and started over. Never mind! It is worth any effort. I checked with my trusty old gardening book, "The Complete Book of Garden Magic" and found nary a word about this tree. However, I learned a lot about the wisteria vine. It blooms in May, requires little care and if planted correctly, will bloom well for you. It must have full sunlight, plenty of rotted manure, plenty of moisture and some bone meal. Seedlings may not ever bloom so it's best to buy grafted plants from a reliable nursery; they often bloom the second year. You need to prune (if it's going to be a vine) to two main stems or not over three or four and top prune during June, July and August. On young plants, remove about one-third of the top to develop side growth. Cut back the side growth monthly on young plants. If you have an old plant which is out of control, prune back in August to within four feet of last year's wood to encourage blooming and to make a dense plant. Sometimes, when an old plant refuses to bloom, it's time to root prune to keep it from going to stems and leaves. This is done by digging a trench, spade deep, all around the plant. Loosen the soil in the bottom and drive a spade down full length, cutting all roots within the circle. Then fill the trench with composted soil. On young plants, the circle should be about three feet from the stem; the circle could range up to six feet for very large ones. Now you know all I have found out about wisterias.

In other cases, failures in gardening come from just plain ignorance. Case in point is the poor man who finally admitted that he just couldn't make his lilac bloom. He said that he had moved it every year to what he hoped would be a better place and still it wouldn't bloom. Someone finally told him that he should have a little patience. A lilac often takes a few years to bloom. In case that man is a reader, I only was told the story, not the man's name.

Some wondrous things happen to gardeners, especially those who have been gardening for many years. For instance, I now have two Necotianas (tobacco flowers) that are perennials. They have come back each year for three years. This variety of Necotiana is the tall pure white with a strong perfume. I can never find the plant in any nursery and have been unable to locate the seeds. So each year, I let the last ones go to seed and just sprinkle them over a flower bed. Little seedlings come up in late April or early May and I can give some away and plant others hither and yon throughout the perennial beds. They give any area a special sparkle with their small white flowers standing on tall stems. They are about 3 feet tall when fully matured and bloom all summer from late May or June up to frost.

Now that you have finished planting perennials to fill those blank spots in perennial beds and annuals here and there, suddenly there's an adder in the garden of Eden. Mildew! Some kind of chewer! Insects! Seems wrong that it should happen just when the plants are looking so fine.

Let's face it-there's no way to have a garden without some pests or disease. We know that insects have a short life span but they multiply; boy do they multiply. And millions of spores can attack one single plant and then spread all over. Also let's face that if you could eliminate all these pests, others would fly or creep in.

There are some things that you can do, however, to keep these bad things in reasonable control.

First, make sure that the environment is right for each group of plants. The right growing conditions are fertilizers, mulch and water. Get rid of all the diseased plants as soon as you see them. Don't put them in the compost, please. That just spreads the spores or bacteria or viruses or whatever you have. Always keep your garden clean and free of debris that falls when you are cleaning up the plants. And, by all means, destroy all such stuff in fall when you are preparing the beds for winter.

You can do one other important thing to prevent spreading disease. If you know you have been working around a diseased plant, clean the spades or scissors so that it's free of dirt and then wipe them with rubbing alcohol. I know that's a little desperate but you can lose many plants if you aren't very careful.

Another way of prevention is to be careful what you add to your garden. Even your best friend may have plants that will spread disease and surely some careless discount stores will spread spores in your garden.

Now there are some other things you can do to make your garden an unfavorable place for pests and pathogens. When you sprinkle to water your garden, you wet the leaves which in turn provide the best place for fungi. The best kind of waterer is a wand attached to a hose. If you must sprinkle, do it in early morning so leaves will dry quickly. Of course, the best system is a drip irrigation system for the gardener who can afford it and will do the work.

Also, fungi thrive on high humidity and poor air circulation so leave space around the plants so air circulates freely.

No matter how much you do to prevent disease and pests, it will happen! So you need to identify the problems before you can do something about them. I find a good gardening book a great tool. Or you can check with your local Extension agent. Just look in the telephone directory under state offices. They are always happy to help you identify your problem. You might want to take a small branch of your plant or at least a leaf.

You can learn to identify some problems yourself. For instance, nitrogen deficiency can cause the lower leaves of a plant to turn yellow. A calcium deficiency can cause leaf tips to curl. Some problems may be caused by two things so, again, check with your Extension Service. They will have your soil tested in the area of the garden that has problems.

You may want to do something drastic such as just pitching a plant that seems to never be free of disease. I have a miniature rose which gives me trouble each year. Always has mildew. Suddenly, this week it occurred to me that I can just dig it up and be free of that problem. And by the way, I will put the whole thing in the garbage.

Also I have found slug trails that lead to a new plant which has leaves almost completely chewed away. I must look for slug bait in the shelf of poisons. I carefully place it under some large leaves, after wetting the soil.

Aphids are easy to spot on new growth of many plants. They produce a sticky "honeydew" which attracts ants. Mealybugs are usually seen on stems and in crotches of plants. The white flies you can spot when they fly up when you shake a plant.

Some things just can't be controlled such as too much rain or some viruses. A plant infected with a virus is sometimes best dug up and destroyed. Some diseases can be controlled by hand picking leaves.

There are some sprays which you can use in extreme cases. I find that one way of controlling disease and fungi at the same time is with a spray of Ortho combination disease and insect control. Always use this spray sparingly, only spraying plants which must be sprayed.

Most gardeners have planted their perennials and bedding plants. They have weeded, seeded and now can turn to other forms of gardening. One of the oldest and most interesting things a gardener can do with flowers in the garden is to make potpourri. The oldest form of that scented collection was to dry rose petals and buds to use in small dishes placed around rooms. If you use this simplest potpourri, you can place some dried rose petals in the bottoms of waste baskets, in closets and even under beds. But the following recipe is a more complicated form of potpourri and more fun:

3 quarts dried rose petals
1 quart mixed materials such as clover blossoms, lavender leaves and blossoms, carnations and any scented blossom
6 cinnamon sticks, broken
¼ cup whole cloves
2 ounces orris root, ground
1 small bottle rose scented oil

A variation of that recipe is to use lemon thyme, lemon balm, any other fragrant herb, leaves of artemisia, dill seed heads, dried orange and lemon rind, clusters of hydrangea, any wild flower, Queen Anne's Lace, sumac seed clusters, etc. All of these items for potpourri must be dried well before adding to your jar. I spread each day's "pickin's" on newspaper in a spare room and after about two weeks, they are ready to add to the jar. Many recipes don't call for salt but I use a generous handful to a gallon. Leave enough space in the jar to be able to shake all those ingredients well for the first two weeks or so.

It's important to pick all ingredients when dry, preferably at midmorning.

Once you make a batch of this wonderful pot-pourri, you will find lots of colorful and scented things to use.

You can find the orris root and the scented oils in craft stores, in drug stores and in specialty catalogs. The orris root is a bit expensive but you use so little that a bottle will last for a long time. You can use large plastic jars such as those that restaurants get. They are happy to give them to you.

This makes a lovely gift when placed in glass containers with a ribbon.

When potpourri begins to fade, squeeze the ingredients and it will release the scent for a short time. You can keep adding the scented oils, and, properly cared for, this potpourri will last for years.

I hope I have given you the incentive for a new hobby.

It seems that flowers are connected to almost all of our major holidays. Memorial Day is no exception. It began with flowers and even though many people have lost the meaning of this holiday and think of it as just another vacation period for car races, etc., it began with flowers placed as a memorial. I had some idea of what Memorial Day was about from my grandmother but decided to get details for those of you who don't know already.

In April of 1866, four women went to a cemetery in Columbus, Mississippi to decorate graves of Confederate soldiers buried there. There were forty Union soldiers buried there also so they put flowers on their graves, too. A local newspaper carried the story which quickly spread throughout the country. It was a very meaningful thing to do since the country was so divided at that time. For Southern women to put flowers on the graves of Union soldiers was such an interesting thing that a New York paper carried the story of that event. The placing of flowers on graves of all soldiers lost in that great war quickly spread and the day was known as Decoration Day but it was first named in New York. The date was later called Memorial Day. In 1971, the date was changed from May 30 to the last Monday in May. Over 200,000 men died in the Civil War and many more were crippled for life.

My grandmother always went to the family cemetery on their farm to clean the graves of any debris and trim any grass that might have grown under the massive maple trees. She carried armfuls of flowers and a bucket of water to place in the jars which always sat beside the headstones. While Ma cleaned the graves, she talked to me about the people buried there. My great-grandfather, Thomas Lewis, and his wife were buried there along with two or three children. It was there I learned about Thomas Lewis, the scout in the Union Army, who rode for the entire length of the war and who came home with a kidney disease from which he suffered the rest of his life. I had trouble associating him with the large portrait of the man with the dark beard and the piercing blue eyes which hung in the "front room" at Ma's and whose eyes seemed to follow me around the room.

Then we trudged to the Ramey graveyard with our bucket of water and jars of flowers to place on the grave of her "dear sister", Susie. As I grew up, I was with Ma less and she was unable to make her trips to the cemeteries, but those early memories and her vivid descriptions of those long dead linger yet. My grandmother was a wonderful storyteller and I learned more Civil War history from her than later in school. She told about her mother-in-law sitting on the front porch of the old house and hearing the big guns at Dover, Tennessee where the Union gunboats were trying to get by the Southern guns which were entrenched on the shore. She described the young Southern soldiers who were firing the guns when a group of Union soldiers came from behind them and how they scattered and ran for their lives. I learned about the hardships of those women left at home to care for farms and children. I have read letters from Ma's father and mother to each other during the war. He was not so dashing as the scout who rode the big roan throughout the war but he served his country just the same. I shivered in the front porch swing as Ma would tell of the guerrillas and Southern sympathizers who came to raid the home and take or destroy everything. Those history book writers didn't have a thing on Ma.

I remember the flowers that were blooming on Decoration Day were mock orange, roses, lilies and honeysuckle.

I have learned a new word in gardening. It's "tenderennials." That's a plant that we treat as annuals but are perennials in the Deep South.

Another word which is often used in gardening books is "ephemerals". They are flowers which come up, bloom, and disappear till next spring or perhaps next fall. One of those is my autumn crocus. They are large leafy plants, whose leaves look a little like a tulip, and are about a foot high now. But in a few weeks, the tops turn yellow and disappear. Then this fall, they bloom as a large crocus, at least four times the size of the spring crocus. They are quite beautiful but I always forget where they are and over plant or dig into the bulbs. Poppies are another ephemeral and you know others.

A new plant which should be interesting is a cross between the old angelwing begonia and wax begonia. Another interesting new plant is the coleus which likes sun. I am anxious to see the new tall coleus. It gets three feet tall and three feet wide. There's always something new in my flower beds which I look forward to seeing bloom. I have a lavender daylily, a new white azalea and a few others. I also have a new butterfly watering bowl. I had never heard of such a thing, either.

JUNE

Nothing is quite so discouraging to a dedicated, hard-working gardener as to find that mildew has attacked in full force. All the rain this spring has brought on the dreaded mildew in some areas that don't ordinarily suffer from fungi. Shrubs such as pink spirea and azaleas are hard hit this spring. This gardener made a "house call" this past week and found a row of azaleas planted along the house as foundation plantings. The whole row was badly damaged by mildew. One of the reasons was that they were so overgrown that air couldn't circulate. That, along with the constant rains this spring, caused a major problem. The only solution was surgery. This isn't what we would like to do but in some instances, it's necessary. Then a good spraying with a fungicide followed by fertilizer for azaleas should do the trick. The problem is that next spring's blooms will be sparse. Then another row of pink spireas, which should be in full bloom now, was also severely damaged by mildew. The same surgery had to be done. Without cutting these plants back, the result would be dropping of all the leaves. If this has happened to you, follow the first spraying of a fungicide with a good spraying every two weeks or so. A good mulch should follow.

Another problem shrub came up this week. A nandina had not grown much in three years and had only one or two tags of blooms. On checking around the base of the plant, the problem was that the plastic covering in the foundation plantings had been put up to the stem with no chance for rain or watering to get to the plant roots. Just simply pulling the landscape paper back about 18 inches and then cultivating, watering and fertilizing should get this sad plant off to a better start.

However, some garden mysteries aren't solved quite so easily. A case in point is a hydrangea which was recently planted. According to the gardener, all the proper things were done. The hole was filled with water, etc. but one little thing was overlooked. While at the nursery, the potted plant was watered but the root ball inside of the pot had not gotten water. It was dry as a bone. The solution was simply to let a slow trickle of water run into the plant for an hour. It perked right up the next day. So when planting something new, be sure that the pot has been thoroughly watered.

JUNE

While helping my sister last week to trim and weed her shrubs, we both kept looking for that dreaded three-leaf plant, poison ivy. At this season, poison ivy becomes a great nuisance. If you find that you have some of this miserable plant, there's a spray just for poison ivy. Or you may have some friend who isn't sensitive to it who will pull it out and off trees. If you happen to be exposed, bathe at once. Do not put any stems or leaves in a compost pile or stand near smoke when burning it. One summer of fighting a case of poison ivy will make these precautions more important to you.

Tomato plants often will drop blossoms when the nights are cool or extremely hot in early spring. To prevent this very disappointing happening, a veritable crisis, spray the clusters of blooms with Blossom Set. And don't forget to give your tomato plants about one tablespoon of Epsom Salts every two or three weeks. That will keep the bottom leaves nice and green plus keep the plant bearing for a longer period.

Another reminder regarding bag worms: check your foundation plants for the bags and pick off any you find that you can reach. If you think the worms have already hatched, spray the whole plant with Sevin, Dipel or Malathion. Don't forget these are killers.

If ever there's a perfect month, it's June. Someone has said, "Our notion of what makes a paradise always returns to the image of a beautiful and fruitful garden". June is the month when it all comes together, all the time, labor and money you spent all year long. But, alas, there are adders in the Garden of Eden. Too much rain and everything gets mildew. Not enough rain and it all looks wilted. Then there are insects everywhere and you wonder what spray to use on what. The truth of this matter is that you can prevent a lot of problems by careful planning. First, a program of spraying for mildew will prevent such an outbreak. Also trimming shrubs and preventing overcrowding of perennials helps prevent mildew. Also removing and destroying yellowed leaves from plants helps to stop the spread of black spot.

Insects are another and sometimes bigger problem. First, you should know that insects are more likely to attack weak, sickly plants. One good way to control insects is to attract birds to your property all year long. Birds are far more efficient than you are at getting rid of the bugs. Those bluebirds, especially, are at work 24-7 cleaning your area of flying insects. I also have seen robins dive down under perennial plants looking for snails and insects on the ground. I often tell the story, at the risk of ridicule, of seeing a robin whacking his beak against the landscape timber around a flower bed. He just kept repeating this strange behavior. On closer inspection, he had been cracking open snails which were all under the leaves of plants.

Slugs are another very hateful pest. They can often be found under hostas and can literally strip a bed of hostas. There is a fine killer of slugs called slug bait or slug poison. It comes in a cardboard container and is in granules which can be placed under landscape timbers and rocks and also under the hostas and other plants where you find the "silver slug trail". Slugs have few predators, and that's understandable, but among those are a few kinds of birds, moles, shrews and SNAKES! Those little garter snakes love slugs.

I realize that snakes play a role in the ecosystem but I don't want them where I am. I have found that each gardener has a different idea of what constitutes an undesirable critter in his or her Garden of Eden. I am terrified of snakes, big or little, venomous or not. Others are afraid of those big, colorful garden spiders which I think are beautiful and wouldn't kill. Other gardeners get upset over the neighbor's cat in the garden. I can't imagine but then I love cats. So bad critters are in the eye of the beholder.

Most of us agree on the most desirable inhabitants of our gardens. Hummingbirds give my whole family much pleasure. We have two feeders that can be seen from our living room and their antics are a constant source of pleasure. There's the big male bully and the different kinds of hummers and now there are tiny young ones all buzzing around the feeders. Having flowers that attract hummers near their feeders also helps to attract them. They love any trumpet shaped flower and especially red, orange or yellow ones.

I also enjoy butterflies and have a variety of plants in my mixed English garden that attract butterflies. First, it's important to have some plants for the butterfly larvae such as parsley, finnel, false indigo, hollyhocks and sedum. The larvae need these plants to feed on. Then the adult butterflies like purple coneflower, coreopsis and especially the Buddlea or butterfly bush.

Having a flower garden with a great mix of flowers has more than one advantage. This mixture attracts fewer insects than a garden concentrating on just one plant. Also you will find that roses scattered throughout a mixed garden are healthier. So you are more likely to attract hummingbirds and butterflies and will have fewer problems from pests and disease if you have a wide variety of flowers. Some flowers in that varied garden, such as marigolds, repel insects. I like to have a few marigolds just for that reason, and when the bloom begins to fade, I cut it and scatter the petals in the flower bed. Some gardeners make a solution of marigold flowers and stems in a bucket of water and water their other plants with the solution. You have noticed, I'm sure, that some plants never have insect problems. Those are usually the ones that give off a perfume that insects don't like such as all the herbs and the strong smelling Russian Sage and Artemesia.

So on with the war with insects and diseases.

JUNE

Often I wonder at this mysterious gene that makes some of us dedicated gardeners and others will quit working in their flowers and shrubs when the weather is too hot or too rainy or too dry or when the diseases show up and insects abound. When I was a very little girl, my mother and I walked to a neighbor's or to Ma's and I had to be constantly reminded not to go off the road to pick some beautiful flower. Where I lived, there were some very nasty venomous snakes and one didn't wander in weeds or tall grass. My dear Ma loved flowers and was forever finding some few minutes to slip out to pull weeds or snip dead flowers. Before her, my great-grandmother was a flower and plant lover. She was an herbalist though she probably didn't know the term. She wandered in the woods and fields looking for special herbs which she used as medicines. She was known to often find some wildflower to bring home or some pretty rock. So I come from a long line of gardeners who are not easily discouraged.

My dream garden would be nothing but flowers and blooming shrubs with no grass, only some paths among the flowers. My grandmother's sister, my great aunt, Angie, was such a gardener. She was a tiny woman and lived in a tiny log house about three miles from my Ma and Pa. She fenced in her yard and had only paths among the flowers, no grass. Her yard was a mass of color and I thought how lucky she was. She lived by a swift, clear creek filled with minnows and interesting things and had all those flowers. Of course, her poor chickens lived outside of the fence, victims of foxes and bobcats, but I didn't know about that. I also didn't know that they had no land and her husband didn't have much of a garden and my grandparents' frequent trips were for Pa to take wagon loads of produce from his big gardens. Nevertheless, I would like a garden just like Aunt Angie's.

Are you finding ants in your flower beds? If so, this is not good. Wherever you find ants, you are likely to have aphids which, of course, you don't want. The following is true: ants will keep a herd of aphids as we do milk cows. I didn't believe this either but checked with a leading horticulturist's book and found it true. Strange things happen in your garden.

Many gardeners are wondering about transplanting. The answers vary with the plants. For instance, to transplant Oriental Poppies, you must move them soon after they bloom when the foliage is wilting a bit. But if you wait too long, they will wither and disappear. To answer those of you who would like to move peonies, don't do it until mid-October or they go into shock and won't bloom for a few years. But you can move daylilies any old time. They are such hardy plants that they can be separated and moved any time during summer as long as you follow the usual directions for transplanting.

It's a good idea to carefully check any new plant you bring into your garden, even those from friends. Plants bought at discount stores may also carry diseases. But let's face it, you can't have a perfect garden of Eden.

Don't forget to add some Epsom Salts to roses and tomatoes. A tablespoon sprinkled on the ground around the plants keeps them green all summer. I like to use it at least every month. I also use it on tall garden phlox if they have yellow leaves at the base of the plant.

You can't win them all. Sometimes the most careful gardeners have plant problems but we persevere!

Those of us who love the outdoors and enjoy growing plants have many things to bedevil us. There's also mildew, thrip, beetles, white flies and the list goes on. Those many critters attack those plants we enjoy but there are critters that attack us! There's the chigger who attacks about the time you're through working in grassy areas. A chigger is about 1/15 of an inch long. They bite where your clothes fit the tightest and they burrow into your skin. They feed and then fall off and are gone before you know they are there. There's the misunderstanding. You never actually see a chigger. That red spot is where they WERE and you itch like crazy. Any anti-itch medicine will cure that. The best way to avoid chigger bites is to use a repellent before you go into their territory and a hot shower when you come in.

Ticks have become a real concern since we know about lime disease and one other disease which the deer ticks carry. This very small tick attaches itself to your skin and burrows in. A spray before going where they might be is good and also the hot shower after-wards. The truth is that it takes more than 24 hours for them to become imbedded. All methods of remov-ing an imbedded tick agree that you must not twist or jerk them. Pull gently outwards and upwards. Then preserve that varmint in a jar in case you have a red-ness of skin around the bite. Then your doctor will know what he is dealing with. Enough of ticks!

Don't neglect mulching your flower beds and shrubs before the hot, dry days of July. Mulch keeps the soil moist and cool and it also keeps the soil soft and able to retain the rain and watering. Remember to mulch peonies very lightly. For some reason, they don't like heavy mulch as most perennials do.

JULY

It seems that in July all kinds of strange things happen to our plants. Even the shrubs and young trees are sometimes fighting a battle with insects. For instance, in early summer, holes seem to come in the leaves of the magnolias. There's a little weevil that's the culprit and they feed in July and drop onto the ground before August and that's when you can kill them. Spray under the magnolias with old reliable Sevin.

Another culprit which often shows up about now is the azalea lace bug. Such a pretty name for something that can cut some really impressive holes in azalea and rhododendron leaves. The leaves will be spotted with specks on the underside. Again, use Seven to get rid of them. It may take more than one spraying with Seven but eventually, they will be gone.

If you are very, very unlucky you may someday find you have the most miserable pest I have ever had to contend with. It has many names. My grandfather called it "dodder". It's sometimes called "lovevine" and old names for it were "strangleweed" and "goldthread". Sound familiar? It's a very thin golden-colored threadlike string that winds around and around plants and it chokes them to death. One year, I brought it into my garden by spreading some dry manure around. It enveloped my asters and many other plants. Every day I spent time pulling it off and burning it. Sometimes, I had to pull up a whole plant. No spray of any kind will kill it. Just time and patience and you might as well put a stool in the garden and plan to spend a lot of time there. Eventually I got rid of it but I always dread finding a tiny bit of it. I found one book that suggested that, once you have picked and pulled it all off, you spray the infested area the following spring with a pre-emergent weed control.

While on the subject of insects, please remember your cats and dogs suffer from fleas and ticks during the summer and only you can help them. Take them to the vet for flea sprays and/or pills and bathe them regularly. On second thought, maybe you might not want to bathe the cat! There are also powders and lotions available.

Your young trees may not make it till spring unless you water thoroughly during hot, dry weather. Keep grass from around them and use mulch, being careful not to let the mulch get up on the bark where insects and mice will have a field day. Lay a hose down in the area around the trees and leave it there for 20 or 25 minutes, moving it from one side to the other. Large trees need more time with a hose and also a wider watered area. In fact, water as far as shade goes because that's how far the roots go. For large trees, a soaker hose is best.

From now until the last of August is the ideal time to start little roses under a fruit jar. It's so simple and so much fun. The easiest to start this way are the tough miniature roses. Also the old-fashioned roses are easy to propagate with the fruit jar. First, enrich the soil where you want to put a cutting. Dig down at least a foot and add compost and some old manure and mix with the soil. Take cuttings by pulling a stem downward leaving the heel on the stem. That's where the roots will start. Leave the cutting in water for several days. Then roll about three inches of the bottom of the stem in rooting compound if you have it. Make an impression in the prepared spot, fill the impression with water and after it is soaked up, put the stem in the hole, being careful not to rub off the rooting compound. Press the soil together and cover with a quart or half gallon jar. I like to surround the jar with two large rocks to keep dogs from knocking it over during the winter. If all goes well, in spring you will have a fine little rose. Leave the jar on the little rose next spring until there is no danger of frost. You will need to leave it in the same place for a year.

I always start at least three of the kind I want because they won't always be a success. Two or three readers have suggested splitting an old potato and putting the stem in the split before planting. That's what my great-grandmother did, I was told. I tried it and sometimes got a lot of potato sprouts. As the potato rots, it provides moisture for the roots. You will need to keep this stem moist all summer and fall. You might want to start them near your water source.

The beauty of garden lilies and the ease with which some kinds can be raised should make them one of our most prized plants even though it's not always easy to keep a planting free of bulb disease. But most of the time, when properly planted, a single bulb sold from $2.00 to whatever you wish to pay, will bloom for five years without further attention, and not one bloom each year but blooms by the dozens after the bulb gets settled.

The name lily is sometimes confusing. Lily-of-the-valley, African-lily, daylily, waterlilies, etc. are misnamed and are so called not because they are part of the lily family but because their flower resembles the true lily.

Not all lilies are adapted to home gardens but a proper selection will give you blooms from June to September. Usually a medium size bulb will give just as good results, or even better, than the biggest bulb. If you have some of the true lilies that are not thriving, after they bloom is the time to move them. I recently had to move some which I had planted in a spot that had had too many rotted leaves added to the soil and that soil was too alkaline. After moving them to a less alkaline spot, they started thriving. Lilies need moderate soil, good drainage and sunshine. Lilies should be planted by October so it's not too late to order. There are two types of true lilies. There's the tiger lily, and a few others which are similar, that you remember from your grandmother's garden. Sadly they are out of favor right now but I have always loved them. They're the old orange with the big brown spots. They multiply from little bublets which grow on the stem and drop onto the ground. If you choose to grow tiger lilies, it's a good idea to choose a spot just for them since they have a tendency, if left alone, to really multiply. The tiger lily is not the plant to mix with perennials in a flower bed. I think it's worth a spot in some corner by itself, however.

Then there's the other kind of lily which multiplies from the bulbs. They include the one which you already know as the Easter lily, the Madonna, Regal, the Star and many others. Most true lily bulbs are planted about four to six inches deep (to the base of the bulb). The Madonna is planted a little less deep. If you want to be successful with this lily, you need to keep a few things in mind. They like neutral soil and no manure. They need moisture on hot summer days just like any other garden plant. They don't like to be moved and since that's necessary only after five years or so, that's not a big problem. They look best, to this old gardener, in groups of three or more of one color, scattered throughout the perennial garden.

Since different varieties bloom at different times, this assures you of beautiful big blooms all summer. They will tolerate some shade but will not tolerate interference from roots of trees and shrubs. Lilies will thrive in clay soil if it's mixed with a little black soil with a little sand added. Mulch is extremely important and some growers will use straw after the ground is frozen. However, I've never lost a bulb from freezes and I just leave the mulch on during winter.

The two varieties of true lilies described above are not to be confused with daylilies even though the blooms look a little alike. Daylilies have fleshy roots and are different in most every way. In fact, daylilies are city cousins of the old, and I think extremely ugly, orange lily which you see at the side of the road. You might call them the old wild lilies of your grandmother's day. I hated them then. I do, however, love the many colors and sizes of the city cousins. In fact, I have several colors of the newest variety, the one which blooms more than once a year. Daylilies multiply much faster than true lilies. Also the daylily doesn't mind being moved at any time and any place.

Lilies, daylilies, tall phlox, veronica, Russian sage, Autumn Joy sedum and a few roses would make an excellent base for a perennial garden. Those would be the plants I would buy first if I were starting a new perennial garden, keeping in mind that the Russian Sage and Autumn Joy sedum like very dry soil and need never be watered. Those few plants would assure you of color all summer and any other perennials could be added to complete a "cottage garden".

JULY

A friend told me that her mother in Germany made a wonderful healing oil by placing the Easter lily bloom in a bottle filled with olive oil. She let it set for some time before taking out the petals. It was used as a healing oil on most everything. She had other remedies made from plants in her garden but that one struck me as most interesting. I had a great-grandmother who also made all kinds of home remedies using her garden plants plus some from the deep woods nearby. One thing she used was foxglove (digitalis) which she used as a medicine for heart trouble. The story of that ancestress was handed down to me and I always wondered how she knew how much and what strength to give. Of course, she didn't know. This great-grandmother made it through the Civil War without a man in the house and raised 8 boys and 4 girls. She was sent for anytime there was sickness in her community and accompanied her doctor whenever he had a particularly difficult case. There was no verbal record of how many patients she lost!

Yes, you can always learn something new. To finish ripening a tomato indoors, place it with the stem side up and a good place to set a tomato to ripen is in an egg carton and you can use both top and bottom of the carton. Do not place a tomato in a sunny window. This hint came from a friend who was visiting us from Minnesota. He's with FIMA and was working in Southern Illinois where they have had floods.

Joe is an agronomist and is a virtual fount of knowledge so I tried the trick with tomatoes and they do ripen better.

Did you know that our common ruby-throated hummingbirds, though native to the East, are found from Canada to the Gulf of Mexico, but their range ends where the Great Plains begin? Other species are found in the West. Did you also know that they must eat almost continuously, only surviving the night by going into a deep torpor to avoid the need for food? A garden with nectar-rich blooms will attract them and their favorite garden plants include bee-balm, cardinal flower, columbine, hollyhock, particularly the red ones, red salvia and trumpet vine. I recently learned that they also eat aphids, mites, spiders and other small insects. The best way to attract them to our feeders is to have one or more of these flowers near the feeders. If you have observed hummers in your garden and are not familiar with the ruby-throated hummer, the male is the one with the bright red throat, an iridescent green back and the forked tail. The female has no red throat. Her tail is blunt with white spots. Poor female!

An old friend, who I hope still reads my column sometimes wrote me that once you begin to observe the birds in your flower garden, you become an avid bird watcher. He was right. It took me years to realize what an important role birds play in the garden. And the bonus is the pleasure they give the gardener.

Now is a good time to propagate Oriental poppies and bleeding hearts. Though the foliage has vanished, dig down until you find the fleshy roots. Cut a section of root into inch long pieces and plant them where the soil is a rich loam with a little sand. Keep the area fairly moist and lightly covered with straw, and soon tiny leaves will shoot up. The new plants will be ready to move into permanent headquarters by next spring. Isn't that an easy way to get more plants? It's nice to have a "nursery" somewhere in your garden and enrich that area to start new plants. It's best to have it near your water source so you won't be tempted to neglect keeping the soil moist. You can also use that area to start new perennials from seeds and to start rose cuttings.

In addition to the above way to propagate, don't forget that you can start new plants In July by layering. Some plants that are easy to start this way are verbenas, pinks, pachysandra, ivy, climbing roses and many flowering shrubs. In fact, all the plants with reaching runners will probably take root if fastened down on soft earth with a wire and covered in a small area, near the wire, with soil. I always put a big rock over the dirt so that the lawn mower won't hit my plant. And, hopefully, not the rock!

The above are very old methods of propagating your garden plants and probably go as far back as man tried to beautify his surroundings. Being a devotee of Western lore, I love to read about the early pioneers going West and carrying starters of fruit trees, vines, and even roses. They kept them moist by wetting them down at every watering hole.

Dig up and burn any stunted and yellow glads. They won't flower and you will prevent infection from spreading in your soil to other bulbs.

Veronica, hollyhock, perennial blue salvia and phlox will all bloom again if kept from seeding.

You may need to water perennial gardens every other day in this hot weather. Some plants which will need more water are hostas, tall garden phlox, roses and astilbe. You may have others which experience will tell you need water more often. Good mulch will help immensely in keeping the soil moist.

Some gardener has said that July is just like June only moreso. It's hotter, wetter or drier. And it's sure that anything that eats plants is moving around in your garden or if not yet, then soon. The sun loving plants are getting too much shade and the shade lovers are getting too much sun and every plant is getting holes from some chewing insect. July is when the battle starts. Late July is also when you look around and wonder why you ever planted so many plants.

August is a good time to start roses under fruit jars so start looking for Rootone, which can be hard to find. Rooting roses this way is a very good way to start miniature roses. I like to start the roses where I want them to grow. Just pull off a branch of any rose so you have a good "heel", place the branches in water for about 24 hours, trim off any blooms and leaves from about 10 inches down and roll the stem end (the heel end) in Rootone and put about 6 inches of the stem under soil. To make a hole, put a shovel in the ground and rock it back and forth until you make an impression, fill with water a few times and you have a place to put the stem. Then press the soil back in place and put a quart or half-gallon glass jar over the stem. If the stem is too long, cut off the top until it fits. Place rocks on either side of the jar to keep it in place. Then keep that soil moist until late fall. Next spring, you will have a little rose. I don't try to move them until they are a year old. My grandmother could take a rose from a bouquet and start it in her garden in the middle of summer. Plants always seemed to know that Ma knew what she was about.

It's super important to keep your azaleas and rhododendrons well watered during July and August because their roots are very shallow. If they aren't well watered during the hottest part of summer, they stand less chance of getting through the winter.

If you have more than two inches of mulch around your perennials, you might need to use a little lime around plants, working it into the soil. Mulch, being slightly acid, may be too much acid for most perennials and can retard growth. Be sure you aren't adding lime to acid-lovers.

Keep your roses well-watered, fertilized and spray them every week or two with a fungicide to keep down black spot.

Deadheading all perennials is very important. That includes roses. About the only perennial that can bear having the flower left on is the astilbe. The dry flower of the astilbe is rather attractive. Since it won't bloom again this year, it won't hurt the plant to leave the bloom as is. Cut off all the spent blooms of daylilies.

The watchwords for July are always high mowing, deep waterings and weed watchfulness. Watering time is here again and we gardeners often fail to water deeply. If in doubt, stick a shovel down a few inches and test for moisture. You may be surprised to find dry soil down about two inches.

Now is the time to sow perennial seeds in some partially shady spot in your garden. The soil should be loose and rich and I suggest having this nursery near water because you will need to water often, both before the seeds germinate and as the little plants grow. Also check Asters for a nasty little bug that attacks Aster tips and spray with a good insecticide if you find some.

Sometime this month when growth has stopped and the vanished foliage lets you know the plants are dormant, dig up a good root each of Bleedingheart and Oriental Poppy. Cut the long roots into inch long pieces and plant them where you have started a nursery with the perennial seeds. Keep the area moist and soon tiny leaves will shoot up. These new plants will be ready for permanent quarters next spring. You can also layer anything with long runners now.

Now, since gardeners are often confused about their care, here are some facts about clematis. First, they like rich, well-drained soil with plenty of lime. They won't grow where you have a lot of oak leaves on the soil because of the acid. They need shaded roots and this is essential and partial shade is also all right for the vine. Cultivation, if at all, must be shallow. They must be protected from winter winds by a thick mulch. A neat little trick is to plant a Hosta beside the vine for shade. You can also stack bricks up about a foot all around to create the shade for the roots. A thick layer of well rotted manure is a good idea. Most varieties bloom in June and July and then spotty blooms the rest of the summer. However, some of the smaller flowering ones will bloom just a bit later but they usually have a fragrance lacking in the ones with the larger flowers. Now we get to the point my friend asked for. Most of the varieties should be treated as a perennial and cut back to the ground each spring unless great masses of flowers are desired. In that case, prune the vine to keep in shape and cut back every three years to strengthen. They require practically no other care. The most popular flowering types are Henryi (white), Jackmani (blue or purple), Madame Eduard Andre (red), Ramona (lavender). Then there are the double whites and the mauve and several others. Jackmani and some others which start blooming in July and continue to some degree until frost should be cut to within two feet of the ground in March to stimulate new growth. Some varieties bloom both in spring and then again in fall. These should have little pruning. Some parts of the vines will winter kill and early in spring we remove any dead wood. As you can tell, there are no hard and fast rules with clematis. The kind of pruning depends on the particular variety. With all kinds, keep the dead blooms cut and keep the soil moist. I have a variety with little white flowers all over and with the fragrance and I wish I could find something to retard its growth. You can almost watch it grow. Then I have the Jackmani which behaves very well though it needs a little more sun. Since I don't plan to move it again, it will just have to make do with what it gets!

By mid-July, diseases and insects start showing up to disturb that garden which you planted so carefully.

Often the leaves of tomato plants start curling. This is a disease, a virus in fact. The best way to avoid tomato diseases is to buy plants which are disease resistant. But if you don't do that, then buy a spray intended just for tomato diseases. In fact, if you really enjoy tomatoes, keep this spray on hand.

Another problem which begins to appear about this time is the brown patches in the lawn. Most of the time, dead patches are indications of undesirable critters. They may be white grubs, the larvae of moths or the sucking insets such as chinchbugs or leaf hoppers. The best way to control these pests is to have a properly watered, mowed and fertilized lawn. The insecticide Diazion works on almost all lawn insects but it must be used properly. Late July and August is the time to control white grubs. Check with your local garden center to find the correct spray for all these pests. However, the grass will not grow back in those spots. You will have to replace the grass. On very small damage, grass will grow to cover the area.

I recently heard of a good way to get rid of white flies, those little flies which swarm up when you disturb a plant. Orthene will kill them but another way is to paint a board yellow since they are attracted to yellow and then paint the yellow board with motor oil or any tacky substance. They are supposed to get stuck when investigating the yellow board.

A good way to keep cut flowers fresh is to add a lemon-lime carbonated drink to the water in the vase. The pop contains citric acid to help prevent bacterial growth and the sugar provides the sugar which the flower loses. Don't use the beverage straight up! Dilute to about half with water.

An experience taught me the value of having good photographs of your landscaping. It's important to have many photographs from different angles of your house. Would you believe landscaping adds 25% to the market value of your house? The damage to your house and plants from falling trees can often be covered by insurance but not without proper photographs. A good place to store those pictures is in the bank safety-deposit box next to your gold and diamonds.

Discontinue fertilizing your trees, shrubs and all perennials about the first week in August. They should not get any new growth when they are getting ready for fall and winter.

You can move Oriental lilies by the end of July and there are some steps to consider. First, the bulbs should be planted about four to six inches (to base of bulb). They must have good drainage. They must be fed a good bulb food and no manure, ever! Throughout the summer, I include them in feeding all other perennials which don't need acid fertilizer. They don't like to be moved and a good gardener moves them only when absolutely necessary. They will tolerate some shade but no invading roots from trees and shrubs. The soil is the most important thing to consider with Oriental lilies. They don't like decaying materials such as old leaves. They do best in soil with a clay base and some added black soil, either from a nursery or your compost. Also add a handful of sand for each bulb and maybe some fine gravel. My grandmother's big group of those large white lilies thrived in very poor soil and little attention. I doubt they were ever moved. Those beautiful flowers were a great delight to me as a little girl. I picked bouquets of them, not knowing that you should not cut the stem because that can kill the bulb. If Ma cared, she said nary a word! Since she had never scolded me for picking flowers, I would have been terribly surprised.

July 4 has always been THE date for the first ripe tomato for tomato experts and I am happy to report that my first ripe tomato, thought small, was fully ripe on June 24. If you think your tomato plant is large, consider the gardener in Lancashire, England who holds the world record for the tallest tomato plant at 65 feet. This plant produced 1,000 tomatoes in 15 months. That's a record to strive for!

Those of us who are striving for weight loss are dependent on the tomato which has virtually no points in the point system of dieting but much nutritional value.

Gardeners are joining the fitness-minded folks. With just a few adjustments, we are getting very effective exercise and having fun at the same time. Hoeing is a wonderful exercise. Weeding, with all that bending from the waist, will take inches off that waist. Activities like mowing the yard and raking grass and leaves will strengthen your muscles and burn up calories. According to the Journal of the American Medical Association, lifestyle exercises can decrease your blood pressure also. For me, working in the flower beds and all other lawn work, takes all the stress out of my day. It's my own tranquilizer. You must maintain an increased heart rate for at least 30 minutes to make workout beneficial and all of us know that we do that each and every time we work in our gardens. Experts in garden exercise have some suggestions. You should use tools that have long handles for that sweeping motion. Keep your back straight and stop to stretch every 10 minutes and stop to rest when you're tired. And slowly bring your heart rate down. So "plant" your feet in your garden and start exercising. I found, long ago, that I need 10 minutes to rest for every hour I work.

A nice tall thermos of cold lemonade and a chair in the shade overlooking the garden is a great incentive to rest.

Hostas begin to lose that freshness of early spring about this time. To keep them healthy, a good watering program is necessary. Most gardeners find that their hostas need to be watered every other day in hot, dry spells. Hostas tolerate a wide range of soils and they do best in slightly acid soil which has been amended with compost, sand, peat moss, leaf mold and composted manures. They need at least two to two and a half hours of morning sun for the rich colors we want. You can plant the rhizomes anytime and plant the large-leaved hostas no closer than two feet apart. Mulch with pine needles if possible, at least for the first year. Young hostas take at least two seasons to mature and must have regular watering. In spring, before growth starts, put down a ring of slow-release fertilizer around the crown, never touching the very center. Hostas need to be separated only every five years or so and it's best done with a very sharp knife. However, it isn't essential to separate your favorite hostas. They look great planted under and around woody shrubs and deciduous trees with slender trunks. There are so many new, beautiful colors and combinations to choose from. Did you know that hostas are the best-selling perennials in America? Remarkably resistant to insects, shade and cold, their leaves range in size from petite 3/4 inch long to giant 22 inches long. Each new one I plant becomes my favorite.

On the other hand, some water-wise flowering plants you might want to consider are purple coneflower, fern-leaved yarrow and sedum Autumn Joy. Most gardeners have purple coneflowers in bloom now or at least by July 1 and they will bloom to September and longer. They are invasive but manageable. They will grow in any well-drained soil under full sun. Sedum Autumn Joy is a succulent perennial with beautiful foliage and spectacular flowers that bloom pale pink in August and gradually change to a dark mahogany by late fall. They prefer full sun and seem to adapt to any well-drained soil. All these plants take very little water and if watering is a dreaded chore, you might consider a garden of all water-wise plants. And there are many beautiful flowering plants which will thrive and bloom with little water. Some that come to mind are yarrow, Russian sage, lamb's ear, grasses and many others.

Some sage has said that July is like June, only moreso. It's hotter, wetter or drier. And anything that eats plants will hit on you sometime in July. The sun loving plants are getting too much shade and the shade lovers are getting too much sun. Most gardeners are finding holes in plants where some chewing insect has been at work. July is when the battle starts.

Watering is my unfavorite chore so I have made a study of methods. It's called the Stagner lazy method. I like best to use a wand and give the plants full force since the wand diffuses the water and doesn't disturb the plant. The wand fits on your hose and can be found in any hardware or garden store and costs around fifteen dollars and lasts for years. Perennial gardens need at least an inch of rain each week so you can gauge the amount for each plant. I like the wand best because I have some plants scattered here and there that don't like much water, such as lamb's ear, Russian sage and Tritomas. If you wonder if everything is getting enough water, place a small spade in the soil down to about three inches and check. Another good way to tell is when the tall garden phlox looks wilted. The phlox is to your garden what the canary was to the deep mines. If they look wilted, everything else needs water. Some plants which need more water than most are ferns, hostas and delphiniums.

Did you know that mulch keeps the nitrates in the soil since nitrates can't be formed at temperatures above 115 degrees? Thus the summer sun can starve your plants. Think of mulch as a parasol that keeps plants insulated and cool and moist.

Check the outside houseplants daily. Most will need daily watering. I once was Ma's water girl, getting water for her porch flowers from a big rain barrel which was near the big open front porch. That old porch was covered in every kind of houseplant she could lay her hands on. I started watering for her as soon as I could reach down into the barrel without going in head first. I knew exactly how much water to put on each plant. That's one way I learned about flowers.

Some of my Oriental lilies, not to be confused with daylilies, are still in bloom and each summer I remind myself to get more bulbs in fall. If you have some, they may need fertilizing now with a low nitrogen fertilizer such as a 5-10-10. As soon as lilies quit blooming, cut the faded flowers to prevent them from making seeds. This is a very important tip: when cutting lilies, cut as near to the bloom as possible. Never cut the whole stem or you could kill the bulb. Just resist cutting those lovely lilies to put in a vase. The time to buy lily bulbs is in summer and the time to plant is this fall. More about planting them later.

Keep a careful watch on hollyhocks, tall garden phlox, veronicas, and perennial salvias. If you will keep them dead-headed, they will bloom again this season. If you want to keep some seeds from any of these, wait till fall and save seeds from the last blooms.

Did you know that you can propagate your climbing roses? Just fasten down a runner on soft, bare soil with a wire and cover a few inches of the runner with soil. An old bent coat hanger makes a good wire to hold the runner in place. You can propagate many plants this way as long as they have long runners or stems. This is a good way to propagate crape myrtles as well as most flowering shrubs. Just forget about them until next spring when you will have a new plant which you can cut loose and plant wherever you like.

Have you bought the box of Epsom Salts yet? Remember that it makes roses, tomato plants and tall garden phlox greener and healthier. Didn't we know that there had to be a better use for Epsom Salts than swallowing it? Some of us have some horrible memories of that stuff.

Don't throw away those used tea bags. Tuck them under perennial ferns outside. I have even made sun tea in a big bucket when they look kind of wan and sick. A little acid fertilizer may be needed now also. Ma always used loose tea and put it on her asparagus ferns on the porch. She also emptied any unused tea from meals on her ferns as long as it hadn't been sweetened.

If you want cannas to bloom a second time, cut back the spent flower stalk. The way to do that is to cut back the old bloom stalk to just above the first set of leaves. Use a sharp knife or sharp scissors. Cannas need lots of water and fertilizer two or three times during the summer. A 10-10-10 fertilizer is fine.

Don't forget to water your compost pile. If you don't have one, start one! It's a wonderful place for potato peelings, peach peelings, coffee grounds, corn cobs and shucks, melon rinds, etc. But best of all, it's a place for the dead blooms and all the cuttings when you straighten up flower beds.

AUGUST

Many gardeners complain that they have no blooming plants in August. There are many plants that you can add to your garden for blooms in summer. There are the tall garden phlox, bee balm, joe-pye weed, aster, chrysanthemum, veronica, roses, lithrium, Autum Joy sedum, butterfly weed, yarrow and all the annuals. Just keep this list in mind when adding some perennials to your beds.

Then there's the beautiful crape myrtle shrub which is in its glory now. There are three heights, ranging from the dwarf to the largest which will grow to 20 feet tall. They are very easy to grow, being almost insect and disease free. They require full sun and moist, rich, well-drained soil. As a great bonus, they bloom almost all summer. If the spent blooms are cut, they will do even better.

The catch is that they can be subject to mildew if not pruned a bit. You need to know a little about the crape myrtle to prune properly. First, NEVER cut the tops back. The kind of pruning which I like best is to prune them as if they were trees. You may have seen this in magazines and in the deep South. First, cut out some of the cross branches and cut out a few of the oldest branches, all the way to the ground. Some readers have told me that they saw this beautiful tree in Louisiana which looked like a crape myrtle and that's what it was. If you want that look, cut out all but four to six of the strongest canes and trim off all side branches up to four or five feet. Thus, a tree! The branches of the large crape myrtles can hang to the ground after a rain or storm and even break from the weight. Trimming them in this way keeps the branches upright.

If you find that your crape myrtle has mildew, spray with a fungicide. Use the trusty sprayer which you use for roses and thoroughly wet the whole shrub. Then repeat this every 2 weeks.

The other method of pruning a crape myrtle shrub is to keep the canes to six or so by cutting them out each spring and by pruning a few of the cross branches inside the shrub. Either way, you have increased air circulation and prevented mildew. Cut back any spent blooms down to the point where the bloom stops.

Crape myrtles come in many colors, from snow white to deep red and all in between. It also comes in three heights.

If you want to fertilize this shrub, use the 5-10-5 which you use for so many blooming plants. Remember that the middle number is phosphate and needs to be a high number for blooming plants. The first number is nitrogen and the last number is potash. Crape myrtles should be free of grass and mulched as any other shrub.

Crape myrtles, butterfly bushes, other flowering bushes and many perennials can fill your garden with blooms during the hot month of August.

Don't let your flower beds get that run-down look as we are so tempted to do in August. Cut out all dead stalks. Keep dead blooms cut. Keep edges trimmed. When plants look ragged, trim them back. When an annual seems to be about through for the summer, pull it up and put it on the compost heap. In other words, neaten up your garden. It will pay dividends in the long run. Remember that every weed that ripens and spreads its seed means more trouble for you next spring.

If you're looking for an easy way to add mulch around trees and shrubs without digging out the grass, I have the answer for you. Put down about 6 to 8 layers of newspaper in the shape you want the mulch, wet the newspaper thoroughly and add about 2 inches of mulch. Leave a few inches around the stem or trunk without newspaper so water will get to the plant. This is the same method you can use when planning a bed for next spring. Now is the time to add the paper in the shape of the flower bed and follow the above directions. By spring, the paper will be decayed and gone and the soil will be soft and easy to dig. I found out about this method many years ago and think it's super.

Stop fertilizing perennials, especially roses, about the second week in August. This prevents new growth about the time they go into dormancy. About the end of the first week of August, give some things a shot of liquid fertilizer and maybe a tablespoon of Epsom salts if they look under par. Then put the fertilizer away for this year. Don't worry about the annuals because they aren't coming back anyway.

Set your mower to 3 inches to protect your grass from August heat.

It would be nice if you could sit back in August and just enjoy the fruits of your labor but sadly, there are things to do and most important, things not to do.

Starting with the things not to do, don't do any pruning of landscape plants now. Once I get out the pruning shears, I can get carried away but restraint is good now. Those landscape plants are getting ready for winter already and don't need any exposed ends. Cold weather could kill them. Once cold weather gets here, you can prune some hollies, magnolias and evergreens. I learned many years ago that the time to prune them is when you want greenery in the house for Christmas. Works out just right.

However, deadheading many of your plants is most important to keep them blooming. Continue to cut off the top dead blooms of tall garden phlox. Deadhead roses, veronica, all annuals and any flowering plant whose blooms are faded. It's most important with roses to keep them blooming till fall.

Continue to hand-pick bagworms and while you are looking for bagworms, check for tent caterpillars that you might encounter in the crotches of trees. Two ways to get rid of those caterpillars are to tear a hole in the webbing and spray with Sevin or cut them down and burn them. Hunt them late in the day when all those caterpillars are back in their little tents.

Evergreens, both broad leafed and coniferous, should be planted from now to September 15. They need a lot of water, so it's most important, when resetting them, to saturate the soil. Where possible, too, let them be protected somewhat from the sweep of drying summer winds

Biennials, such as foxglove, can be started from seed now. Set out any young plants in the border for the winter would probably kill them. Be sure to shade those seedlings.

About this time of the year you may discover many self-sown seedlings from hollyhocks, larkspur, columbine, sweet William, etc. If you like the parent plant, these should be carefully guarded because this is a great way to stretch your garden budget. Remember that phlox seldom come true to color from seeds.

If you have a tall garden phlox which you value, remove the seedlings from around it since these seedlings can smother out the parent plant and all you will have is the magenta colored plant which you often see. I still like the old fashioned magenta phlox and plant them in some back garden space. Divide phlox in early September (four or five stalks to a clump) using outside pieces. Have soil thoroughly enriched, deeply dug and conditioned. Remember that to make the best showing, tall garden phlox look best planted in groups of three or more of any one color.

Too few of us think about beautifying cemeteries. Once large cemeteries were landscaped to become famous for their beauty. My local cemetery is plain to the point of ugly! One idea is to plant some perennials which require next to no care such as daylilies and peonies next to a headstone. You would have to surround them with a little metal fence to keep them out of the way of the weed whackers. Another idea is to plant daylilies around the base of trees and in traffic islands such as those seen in Paris, Kentucky. Another planting could be daffodils and grape hyacinths since they can live for years untouched and are impervious to little rodents. Some trees which would live for years and years are oaks, beeches and ginkgos.

If you have poor garden soil for your vegetable garden, consider planting a "cover crop". This adds organic matter to the soil and, depending on the crop used, may add nitrogen to the soil. Check with your local agriculture advisor for a good cover crop. He most likely will advise a legume. Also, save all your fall leaves for use in the paths in your vegetable garden. Eventually those leave will be added to the soil also.

If you have any wood ashes left or if you have some from a burn pile, spread them around phlox, cosmos and especially asters. You don't need to pile the ashes but sprinkle them on the ground near the roots, allowing a little brown soil to show through.

If you put some houseplants outside for the summer, take a good look at them now for insects and keep soil moist. A friend took her lovely Boston ferns indoors a few years ago and awoke a little green snake which poked its little head up in surprise at having its nap disturbed.

Every gardener could write a book entitled "Mistakes I Have Made." This is a good time to check over your flower beds and decide what you could do to improve things. For instance, there may be a bald spot where something died or perhaps a plant just grew and grew and has taken over in another spot. Get out your camera and get a good picture of all the flowers. Next spring, when you are planting and moving plants around, you can improve the whole bed.

Another mistake most of us make at some time is to plant things like Hostas where they look best but they require a lot of water and should not be grouped with something that likes a dry soil such as Lamb's Ear or Red Hot Poker. Again, next spring you can rearrange the moisture lovers together. The picture will be invaluable because we forget where our problems were by spring. A little careful planning will also take some of the work out of gardening. Some of us like a bed with all plants which like dry soil. Others try to combine plants, making for more careful watering.

Avoid adding any quick-acting plant food to roses at this time. A light dusting of bone meal raked in is good. This bone meal doesn't necessarily improve the quality of fall flowers but it is sure to give the rose plant more vigor and strength for blooming next spring. Be sure that your roses have enough mulch at this time. Continue a spraying program with a combination spray for insects and diseases. Your roses need a little extra care during August's hot, dry weather.

If you have thought of taking some garden plants inside to provide for fall blooms, use a sharp knife to root prune them now to a size just a little smaller than the pot. Remove all buds and flowers and cut back the top growth severely. Water well until ready to lift. This is a fun way to continue to have blooming plants indoors for a long period.

Continue a spraying program for phlox and other perennials which are subject to mildew. A plant which is attacked by mildew is weakened before going into fall dormant period. Spores are blown into this area during August from the deep South. That's what I have read and it seems that August is when mildew is at its worst in my garden.

Check your local nurseries for sales of evergreens, both broad leaved and coniferous. They can safely be planted from now to mid-September if you are careful to saturate the hole you prepare for planting plus the root ball and then water again after planting. It's also a good idea to give them some light shade during August with its hot winds.

Hedges of all types and any plants that you keep clipped should be gone over now as growth for this season is about to cease. One secret to success for these plants is to never let them become unkempt and out of control. And do NOT fertilize them now or new growth will start which will winterkill. I have such a hard time trying to keep my boxwoods under control and at the height I want them. It requires clipping twice a year. Since I have about 10 boxwoods, it can become quite a chore. It's not the clipping, it's the cleaning up afterwards!

Have you noticed the many pink "magic lilies" or maybe you know them as "surprise lilies" or "resurrection lilies" or even "naked lady"? This beautiful lily is an amaryllis that has large green leaves that emerge in spring and die back very soon. Then they bloom in August. They seem to bloom at a time when they are most welcome. They are extremely hardy and reproduce at a fast pace. They will grow in full sun or partial shade. They are large bulbs so should be planted at least five inches deep. When the blooms have faded, trim off the dying blooms and fertilize them. They must be very tasty because something ate mine. I have many squirrels and I blame them.

Another idea for cemeteries regards those concrete pots near the headstone. Try planting some ornamental grasses that return every year or even the sedums will thrive. Also, another suggestion is to plant American hollies where the sun will catch their berries in winter. They will grow in the typical clay soil of Kentucky. To sum up, we take flowers to cemeteries to try to make them a more comforting place so why not make some permanent improvements with plants that will live for a long time.

There's a great little booklet called "Kentucky Snakes" put out by Kentucky Department of Fish and Wildlife Resources. It is a most useful booklet even for us old-timers and certainly good for people new to Kentucky. It's free by calling 1-800-858-1549. You might want to ask for their other booklets on fish and wildlife.

Every gardener wants to grow those beautiful blue big-leaf hydrangeas and some tips may be just what you needed to know. First, hydrangeas are well suited to most areas of your garden, as they tolerate both full sun and partial shade. They fit well in shrub borders, or as single specimen plants. They thrive best when planted next to a fence or house where they will be sheltered from winter weather. They are perfect for bordering the edge of natural, wooded lots because they will thrive in partial shade. Groundcovers, such as ivy or periwinkle, provide a plush carpet for hydrangeas. This lovely plant likes rich, moist soil so if soil tends to be dry, be sure to water regularly. In spring, apply a balanced slow-release fertilizer at the base of the plant. In late summer, after blooming, prune stems that bore flowers to just above the nearest outward facing bud. Leave new shoots uncut. Alter the color of blue and pink hydrangeas by changing the soil acidity. Add aluminum sulfate for blue blooms and lime for pink. Prune back old or damaged growth in late summer while the leaves are still on. Early fall is the best time to plant new hydrangeas. Mulch well with shredded pine bark to prepare the plant for winter. Powdery mildew may attack your plant in summer. It appears as a white powder on the leaves and causes them to turn yellow and eventually wilt. Remove the infected parts and spray with a fungicide which is listed for use on mildew if the condition becomes severe. There are several varieties of big leaf hydrangeas. They include Bluebird, which has lacecap blooms, Hortensia-type blooms, Forever Pink and the one which we most admire, the Blue Bonnet. Hang a bunch of the flower clusters upside-down in the kitchen for a lovely, dried flower bouquet in winter. As cut flowers, they make a lovely arrangement. Add a bit of detergent and a teaspoon of sugar to water to make them last longer. One last bit of advice I got from the owner of a nursery: buy the plants in bloom to verify the flower color and be sure the plant isn't diseased since disease could infect other plants in your garden. Now you know everything about the big-leaf hydrangeas that I know!

What causes the bottom of tomatoes to turn brown and leathery? It is a common problem and is caused by calcium deficiency and moisture fluctuation. So water regularly and apply calcium.

When arranging fresh flowers, crisscross the top of a vase with clear tape, leaving openings for stems. This makes flower arranging a breeze.

When repotting plants, put coffee filters in the bottom of your flower pots to allow for drainage and keep the dirt in the pot.

Put water in saucers from clay pots and place them in flower beds to encourage toads. Hopefully, without little garter snakes, you will have lots of toads and no earwigs. Earwigs seem to like certain plants and toads will eat them along with other insects that plague you.

To get rid of mosquitoes, put some water in a white dinner plate, add a couple drops of Lemon Fresh Joy dishwashing detergent. Put the plate on your patio. Whatever attracts the mosquitoes, the white plate or lemon smell, they flock to it and fall dead in the water or on the floor. Works inside your house too.

Don't forget to freshen your birdbath daily. Those birds help your garden by eating insects and their cheerful chatter and antics also brighten your life. One of my favorite pastimes is watching the hummingbirds that feed just outside our den window. They are well worth the trouble of changing their water every 3 or 4 days.

Want to make houseplants of your favorite impatiens? Just cut the tips, remove the blooms and put them in damp potting mix or even a glass of water. They will root in a few days and begin to bloom soon after. They make a nice winter addition to those green plants.

You can have geraniums indoors, too. Start them in pots outside, keep them trimmed back a bit and wash well before bringing them inside for the winter. The older bright reds are the best for this treatment.

Keep your small gardening tools in an old knapsack. All of those trowels, gloves, scissors, string, etc. will be in one place. Hang the sack on a nail in your garage or shed.

If you just can't make yourself become enthusiastic about getting out in your flower beds and working in the hot, dry month of August, don't feel that you're alone. It's just not as much fun as it was earlier. So, to have an attractive garden in August takes some planning.

Plan to spend a few hours in your garden some early morning to spruce it up. First, clean up all dead leaves and broken stems from the beds. If annual stems are lying on the ground, just pull them up for the scrap pile. Any dead or diseased plants need to be pulled up for burning. The idea is to not leave clutter on your flower beds to spread disease. Many of the stems of perennials which have fallen over can be salvaged by staking. It's worth a try. To make this cleanup easier, take along a wheel barrow, a sharp hoe, stakes and string for tying up perennials and I usually drag along the hose for watering when the cleanup is done. While you're in this cleaning mode, dig up any stray grass (and there will be some) and weeds. If you're working just after a rain, it's easier to pull grass and weeds. Just get the roots.

Now is the time to plan for next year's flowers and shrubs. If you plan to move a large plant, shrub or perennial in fall or early winter, it's a good idea to root prune now. Using a sharp spade, cut down as far as the spade will go, about a foot or so from the plant or shrub stem. Make the same cut all around the plant, without removing any soil. You are cutting the small feeder roots to cut down the shock of transplanting. I do this to all perennials if I plan to move them in a month or so. My mother was always in awe of my father's stepmother who could move blooming plants from the back to the front of her house and vice-versa at any time she chose. I learned as an adult gardener that she kept the side roots so short that it didn't cause much shock to the plants. I didn't admire her for much else but she had the most beautiful flowers and they always seemed to be in bloom. Of course, they weren't so pretty around back.

Part of planning is often making a new flower bed or increasing the size of existing ones. A lazy gardener's way is to put many layers (5 or more) of newspaper in the exact shape you want the new beds or larger older beds. Wet them down well and put at least 3 inches of mulch on top of the paper. By next spring, all the grass will be dead and the ground will be soft and easy to cultivate. You can just make a hole where you want to plant instead of digging up the whole bed. Or if you are a glutton for punishment, dig up and enrich the whole bed.

If I were starting a new garden, I would choose a base of a few lilies, some daylilies, several tall garden phlox, veronica, Autumn Joy sedum and a few roses scattered among the other plants. Keep in mind that the Autumn Joy and the Russian sage like very dry soil and rarely, if ever, need to be watered. Those few plants will assure you of some color all summer and other perennials could be added later to complete a "cottage garden."

It's time for you to do something serious if you want that perfect lawn, the envy of all the neighborhood. The following information for an old lawn that needs some repair work and also for the lawn started from scratch. Most of this information can be found in your friendly extension service but maybe reading here will be easier.

If you are starting from scratch, it is suggested that you use tall fescues such as Falcon and Rebel II. Blue grass sounds like it would make a great lawn but is not best for a good drought-resistant, all around grass such as the above. Another idea is to kill all existing grasses with Roundup, allow about two weeks and rake well or till the whole area. I have a neighbor who scraped the lawn clean of all that dead vegetation before seeding. They did this in the spring and now have a gorgeous lawn. Granted, they only have a small front lawn to work with and a devoted gardener who watered regularly. You can also till the soil to prepare a bed for the seeds. If you don't want to use the Roundup, till thoroughly and seed. If you sow in mid-August, you should have a beautiful lawn next year.

If you have a lawn with ugly bare spots or spots with diseased grass, use a very heavy rake and pull out all the dead grass. The idea is to give the seeds a chance on bare soil. That old idea of seeding your lawn on top of snow is "for the birds" and just doesn't do a thing for your lawn unless the grass gets to bare spots. The fellow who sells grass seeds must have started that tale.

Now if you are unfortunate enough to have a lawn of poor bare soil from which the topsoil has been scraped, as for a new house, you have a lot more work to do. Either get some top soil spread on top of the bare clay or enrich the clay. Use large amounts of peat-moss or compost, preferably, and work it in.

The most important part of this business of sowing grass seeds is to water, water, water. You need to water well and deeply to keep the soil moist for at least three weeks or more. Those tall fescues will grow about anywhere but they have to be watered often to grow that lawn you want.

The best thing you can do before planting seeds is to get your soil tested and add whatever is needed rather than guess and use too much or too little of the additives. Whatever you decide to add, use a rotary seeder to get uniform results.

Once the soil is seeded, rake lightly and then mulch with some clean straw. That step is also very important to protect the seedlings.

Once you have grass, mow that young grass with a grass catcher which will pick up some of the straw and the clippings. Keep the mower blade at 1 ½ to 3 inches. Say you want to fertilize since you have made all this effort? Use a high-nitrogen fertilizer and use it sparingly after you have a lawn started.

Now, after all this work and expense, you will probably wish you had bought some first quality sod. If you insist on laying the sod yourself, get some expert advice because it takes a lot of know-how to lay sod properly. Personally, I think it might be cheaper in the long run when you consider all the things you buy.

A list of fall vegetables to plant in late August or early September includes lettuce, mustard greens, spinach and turnips. That reminds me of the time our daughter was invited to a boyfriend's house in a Northern state and called me to exclaim, "Mama, you won't believe it! They eat the turnips and throw away the tops!"

One chore that you might want to consider now is to mark the spot for planting those fall bulbs. In fact, you might even work the soil and add a little fertilizer. The time to plant tulips is about Thanksgiving time and it is COLD to work outside so get some of that work done now.

SEPTEMBER

Now that summer is drawing to a close, there's not much you can do about this year's garden but now is the time to make plans for a better garden. Get after the evergreens, order new roses, order those bulbs you wish each year that you had planted, clean up the flower borders and a host of other fall tasks.

Even if we have occasional rains, remember that the soil dries out quickly now. See that any newly planted or transplanted items are kept moist. They are getting their first root growth now and need a constant supply of water.

Before the leaves begin to fall, get your garden on paper. Now is the time to plan changes which you expect to make during the winter.

Transplanting peonies gives most gardeners cold chills. There's that fear that you will do it wrong somehow and lose your plant. Here's the low-down. Get this job done about September 15, in case you need a deadline. That's about the last safe time to transplant. Only do a few each year so you won't risk losing blooms on all of them.

To successfully transplant peonies, keep a few things in mind. They need a sunny location without roots from trees or shrubs. They will bloom in medium soil but respond best to well-prepared soil. Prepare the holes in advance. Dig a hole more than 12 inches and fill with soil well mixed with perfectly rotted manure and coarse ground bone meal. Tamp this soil down and soak it for several days before planting. This idea is probably new to you in transplanting but works well with peonies. Now prepare the top soil with a few handfuls of wood ashes and a bucket or two of humus.

Carefully remove the old plant, trying not to bruise the tender roots. Allow the root ball to be exposed to the sun and wind for a few hours until the tops wilt. Roots will then be more pliable. Wash off all soil with a hose and cut back the tops to two inches. Cut out any diseased roots. Bend the large clump carefully to find the weakest part and divide there. Each new plant should have at least four or five eyes. When planting, the crown of the plant must remain at exactly two inches from the surface. All soil should be firmed with the fingers and fists. Aren't those your best tools anyway? Water during this procedure to settle the soil. A big point to remember is that a root planted too deeply may not bloom next year or even the next. Now you know everything I know about transplanting peonies. If you are buying new peonies, remember that the most expensive may not be the best. It may just be the newest. Some old varieties are very fine and not so expensive.

Many gardeners like to plant perennials in fall and if planted early enough to get roots established before a freeze, this works well. If you plant too late, you're just "heeling them in" for winter.

I am often concerned that my friends who are not native to Kentucky don't realize that many venomous snakes are active in fall. My dear, wise grandfather always said that copperheads come out of hibernation in March before rattlesnakes and go into hibernation earlier in fall. He was most careful to wear "gum boots", high topped, loose rubber boots when out in the woods at any time of the year but was mindful that he could walk up on a rattlesnake quite late in fall. All venomous snakes in Kentucky are pit vipers. That is they have pits on each side of their heads. They also have vertical pupils. That little tidbit of information is for those who get close enough to notice. The diamond shaped head is not always an indication of a venomous snake. Neither does a rattler always rattle.

I mention these snakes because fall weather does not mean you should be less careful. A friend of mine told me recently of being in the water with a copperhead this summer. By that, she meant he swam right over her body. She was familiar with the copperhead having lived in copperhead country in the deep South and having treated many snake bites in a large Army hospital. A cottonmouth is not always in the water and the others aren't always on dry land. Three of the four venomous snakes lived and thrived on our farm and were just another part of our environment but we learned early to "mind where you walk" as Ma would say.

It's moving time again; well, it's moving time in my flower beds. It's been said of me that I move every plant at least once a year but that isn't quite so. But, when I look around at my plants, I always find some that were planted in the wrong location. Too much sun or too little. In a few days, when it's cooler, a nandina has to be moved and some blooming perennials which just sit there doing nothing because they don't get enough sun. I'm sure all gardeners know the story. Also I have found just the right place for a couple of azaleas which I get to shop for.

Be sure to water your foundation plantings thoroughly before they go into winter with dry roots. More good plants are killed because they didn't get enough water in the fall than from the harsh cold winter. The same can be said for all perennials.

Do not cut back your perennials too soon. Wait for a killing frost when the leaves turn brown. However, pull up those scraggly annuals any time that suits you. Just don't put any in your compost that have mildew. Believe it or not, that mildew can carry over till spring when you put compost on your beds. If cold weather catches you with perennials standing like brown sentinels, never fear. Nothing will happen if you have to wait till spring to cut them down. I always forget to cut down the daylilies. They just sit there and wait for me to cut them back in spring. They also make a nice place for the early garter snakes to hide. It's easy to forget how early garter snakes come out of hibernation. I have no trouble remembering that copperheads come out in March. That's information that all kids knew who grew up where I did.

Have you bought some bulbs and wonder when to plant them? There's an old rule of thumb that hyacinths should be planted when the maple leaves begin to turn color. That's very old but works.

Give your rhododendrons and azaleas one more mulching. Oak leaves or pine needles are best.

Someone asked me the other day if I plant by signs. The only sign I use is to watch for the sap to go down in perennials or shrubs. It took me a long time to catch on. Pa always made such a big to-do about the sap rising and falling and I finally got it. For instance, the reason for fall planting of perennials is that in fall the cooler air causes the flow of sap to stop and the plant no longer concentrates on making green leaves and blossoms but concentrates on the root system and all this activity takes place while the top gradually dies down. However, if you disturb the root system in transplanting, you have to give it time to recover before freezing and before the spring reversal of demands. As long as the ground temperature stays at 40 degrees or better, the root system continues to grow. Next spring, the plant will suddenly be called on to produce green leaves and flowers before any underground activity takes place. So it's good to have strong roots at this time. Next spring, when the weather is warm and we have the urge to plant or move something is a bad time to move shrubs and plants and now you know why. Many times, spring transplanted perennials will live a month or two and die. The demands of the top growth are just too much for the newly disturbed root system. So if you have some things you want to move, get out there and get at it in September.

Watering all perennials at this time of year is ultra important. But it's especially important for azaleas and rhododendrons, roses, astilbe, hostas and tall garden phlox.

This is the time of year when I had to climb up in Ma's attic for her if I was visiting. Pa's popcorn had to be hung on the rafters, along with Ma's brother's Spanish War uniform and some ancestor's violin. There were guitars and bass violins and over in the corner was Ma's grandmother's trunk with all the fascinating things locked inside for a rainy day. On the floor of the attic would be sweet potatoes on newspapers and peanut vines were hung on the rafters to dry. And along one wall were stacked many, many books. That old attic was a wondrous place for a little girl. The stairs to the attic were narrow and winding and my young legs made short work of carrying things up for Ma. I hope you have memories of an old attic. And I truly hope you had a Ma.

Anyone can enjoy gardening in spring and early summer when everything is at its best but it takes a real dedicated gardener to enjoy gardening during a dry August and September. And usually it takes deep pockets to keep watering enough. Most of us water just enough to keep everything alive. The well-established plants do best but the real secret to good plants, even during a dry spell, is mulch. No perennial garden can do without a good mulch. Three inches of mulch has saved many a flower bed. Mulch, besides saving the soil from drying out, makes it easier to get water down into the soil.

A good worthwhile project for September and October is to get ready to pile dirt around your roses. When it's time for this job, it's always so cold so if you pile dirt or mulch near each rose, it will be there to use when the ground freezes and that's when you need to make that mound around each rose. Be sure that the dirt comes from somewhere other than around the rose. You don't want to disturb the rose roots. If you're like me, you won't enjoy getting out in a freezing wind to work on roses.

Fall is "in the air." In fact, fall seems to have a special smell. Some of us are old enough to have special memories of falls of long ago with the wagon loaded with pumpkins going to the hog pens and the big disk cutting down all leftovers in the garden. All the watermelons and cantaloupes brought in before the first frost. The dried beans and peas that were piled up in grass sacks to be hulled later. And oh, how that pricked the fingers. My little fingers could make short work of that chore but would be cut to ribbons. Then there were the big piles of black walnuts drying and later the fun of cracking those walnuts for Ma's wonderful cakes. My grandfather was a man who took great pleasure in gathering berries and nuts for Ma. We had hazel nuts, walnuts and hickory nuts and he grew popcorn and made molasses, all just to make life more pleasurable. Do you remember popcorn balls made from home made sorghum molasses? On the farm, life was just as busy in fall as in summer. Pa had a big orchard and all that fruit was used in some fashion before frost. So many things to do. But I remember that, though they were busy with many chores, Pa had time for reading and Ma always had time for her quilts and they both read The Courier Journal from front to back every single day. And they always had time for their little granddaughters.

Now that you aren't mowing so often and it seems that you can rest on your laurels, or whatever you rest on, tisn't so. It's not too late to start a fall salad garden with lettuce, spinach, mustard greens, radishes, onions and kale. Just a few square feet can give you many fresh vegetables for October.

Believe it or not, it will soon be time for fall fertilizing of broadleaf evergreens but DO NOT fertilize until after the first killing frost. You don't want to encourage new growth.

It's getting near time to dig your glads, dahlias, cannas and tuberous begonias. Get the glads dug just after the leaves turn yellow and the rest before a killing frost. After digging, remove the foliage and let them dry for a week or so. Then store them in peat moss or sand in a dry, cool place. But don't let them freeze. Check them periodically throughout winter and throw out any soft or moldy ones.

Don't neglect to water your azaleas and rhododendrons. One reason these two don't bloom in spring is that they weren't watered enough in fall.

If you want an early start on some annuals next spring, try sowing some of the hardy varieties this fall. Some of these are larkspur, poppies (the annual kind), sweet alyssum, ageratum, cornflower and cosmos. If they come through, you will gain considerable time; if not, the seed lost will amount to little.

Practically all asters need constant division in order not to deteriorate in the garden. Clumps should be divided every year leaving not over five stalks to a plant. They all should be staked early in spring.

Don't feed roses from now on, but they should be sprayed after each rain with a fungicide to prevent black spot and also continue to keep them well watered and mulched.

Magnolias, dogwood and birches do better if spring planted.

I had a dark red, almost black, sweet William pink (carnation) this summer and gathered seeds and planted them about a month ago for flowers for next spring. They are thriving and are about 4 to 6 inches high now. Now I will have a continuation of this beautiful plant for tucking here and there in the perennial garden. These are biennials and must be planted this summer for flowers next spring. It isn't much trouble for the beauty of the color you like.

Here's a little trick to having just the color of hollyhocks you liked this year. Find just the right color and protect the bloom with a plastic bag while the seed is forming. All this to keep out the marauding bees. Save that seed for the plant color you like.

OCTOBER

October is the month for those who love Indian summer and for the children who roam through the neighborhood dressed like ghosts and goblins and sometimes fairy princesses. It's also the time when grown ups can sit back and enjoy a little break from gardening and think that another year has passed and aren't we all glad we're still here. It's also time to enjoy the reds and golds of the woods. This is the time of year when my mother's three daughters took her for a day's outing, looking at those wonderful changing colors which she loved. I will forever think of her when I see fall colors in the woods.

One of the pests we have to contend with in the late fall and winter is the pesky rabbit. Seems Brer Rabbit does considerable damage to young trees.

Wrapping the trees is the best way, of course. A wire cage surrounding them is another way. You can keep rabbits off young beans and peas in spring by sprinkling them with baby powder, not talcum, but the real baby powder.

Incidentally, if you are planting trees or shrubs this fall, don't drive a car or truck across your lawn because it damages the lawn by compacting it. In fact, try not to walk on the lawn when possible. If you do have a compacted lawn, you can rent a funny looking device that is called an "aerator" and which has spikes that drive little holes all over the lawn.

It's time to bring in those tomato plants, if they have survived, to hang in a dry storage area or shed. I once brought some vines into the basement only to find many little flying critters had come to life in my basement. They are called white flies and you don't want a basement full of them. Or keep the ripest ones at room temperature and they will ripen in abut a week. The mature green ones can be spread out in a single layer out of the light. They will ripen in a few weeks if kept at near 70 degrees. Some folks wrap each tomato in old newspaper which seems a lot of trouble but in a month or so, you will be so glad! I have also heard, but haven't tried it, that you can put the tomatoes in a Styrofoam cooler with a couple of apples which promote ripening.

The frost will soon be on the pumpkin but, more important to me, the frost will soon be on the turnip greens. It's something we Kentuckians know from childhood and not very important to newer Kentuckians. I recently had some wonderful turnip greens at a small family reunion and the cook of this wonderful dish said that she had to cook them a long time since they were early fall greens. It took some time to explain this to my husband. And, of course, she had added pieces of jowl and had cooked them in an iron kettle. It's "everyone to his own notion".

Several readers want to know how and when to trim back their hydrangeas. To answer some of their queries, the blue and pink kind which we all love can be cut back only in a very special way so take heed! Remove the flower heads and cut out the old branches which have died but remember that if you cut out the live branches or trim them back, you will lose blooms for next year. Then there is the hydrangea PeeGee which should be trimmed back to two to four buds, or leaf clusters, on each shoot. This is the one which has white blooms and there is a big difference in how you treat them. Both make wonderful dried flowers.

Now on to how to trim back your butterfly bush. In the first place, this is a delicate plant to grow in our climate so you will lose some no matter how you treat them. Be sure they have been watered thoroughly before they go into winter. That's number one. As to how to trim, there are two schools of thought. Some gardeners don't trim them until spring and then cut back to about a foot. I trim mine back to a few inches as soon as they have gone through a hard frost. I have two different opinions from two different gardening books.

If you have a mockorange which has gotten out of control, as they seem to do, and needs some trimming, remember that next year's blooms will come on shoots which grew this year. So the best cutting should be to remove some of the oldest stems, all the way to the ground, to give you a stronger plant and more blooms next summer.

This is a wonderful time to start a compost heap if you don't have one. You can use that big pile of leaves and all the perennial tops. How to start a compost heap is a whole column in itself but a very simple one can be started by clearing a space of grass and weeds somewhere in a hidden spot. Then put all this fall's waste in a heap. You can then start putting kitchen waste on it. Just remember to not use any cooked kitchen waste and no citrus. By spring you can start adding some soil.

Hardy, or perennial, asters can be as beautiful as chrysanthemums for fall color. Most of them came from the wild ones and have been improved long ago. Though they are very popular in England, they have fallen from favor in this country for some reason. One problem in growing asters is that they must be divided most every year in order not to die out. The very tall ones must be staked early or they fall all over the place. The true aster always has a yellow center so, though they come in many heights, you can always tell a true aster. The dwarf ones make a very fetching addition to perennial gardens and some varieties even bloom as early as July. You may have to order aster plants but I think they are worth a spot in your garden. The aster is a good plant to add to your "must try" list.

If you find some bags on your shrubs from the hateful bag worm, about all you can do now is to pick them off and make a note to start a spraying program next spring.

Late October is the time for winter protection of roses but much preparation can be done ahead. A great time for planting roses is anytime from now to freezing. Prepare the beds now if you plan to buy some roses this fall. Keep up the spraying for mildew.

If you have planted some young trees this year, DON'T fertilize them until they are at least a year old.

If squirrels are a nuisance around your house, try placing used kitty litter in bags with some holes cut to let out the odor. For some reason, known only to squirrels and squirrelologists, they hate the smell of used kitty litter. Well, who doesn't? Hang these bags from trees and hopefully the number of trees will equal the number of cats you own, or that own you. Also you might try just emptying the cat boxes around the trees.

All those bulbs that you have been thinking of planting should be in the ground by mid October.

Well, maybe a week or so more. That is, all those bulbs BUT tulips. They should not be planted until late November. The way to remember when to plant tulips is to remember to plant them at Thanksgiving. The small bulbs can be planted by October 1. However, if you still haven't planted them, get out and plant them now. If you forget to plant them, you might as well throw them away. They won't keep till next year. Why not make a trip to the nursery now and buy some very unusual bulbs just for a novelty. There are some very spectacular ones on the market. If you are a patio gardener, you can still plant bulbs in pots just as in the garden. The container should be at least a foot deep. Then plant bulbs as usual and at the usual times.

While on the subject of bulbs, a few words of advice are in order. A good rule of thumb as to the depth to plant is plant about 3 times deeper than the bulb's length and please, pointed side up. While you're digging the holes, put in a little bone meal. But remember, the most important time to feed bulbs is in spring, just as they are coming up.

Those tough jonquils are very rewarding and some great ones can be found everywhere now. When you pass some place where a house once stood, the last sign that someone once lived there is the narcissi or jonquils. I always wonder who the gardener was and when she lived there.

Do you wish, every spring, that you had planted some azaleas? Well, now is a good time. For one reason, the nurseries don't like to carry them over till spring. Try making an offer and you might be surprised at how quickly that nursery owner will deal. They are great plants to tuck into bare spots in shade gardens. There's always room for a few.

When chrysanthemums are through blooming and begin to look like a big bird's nest, it's time to do something about them. Cut them back to within a few inches from the ground. This will help root development and make them send up vigorous sprouts next spring. Next spring is the time for potting them for another fall show. If you have them in a pot and are wondering what to do with them, find a spot in your garden for them till spring. It's good to have the place already dug for them and well watered but by all means, save them. If you want nice plants for next year, keep the mums watered well now. And do not fertilize this fall.

It's time to bring your house plants inside for the winter. They should not be outside when the temperature drops to 55 degrees. If I were you, I would look carefully for little green snakes who like to hide in the foliage. But maybe you are braver than I.

If one of your houseplants seems to be too big for its pot, it needs repotting before settling down for the long winter. Choose a pot that's only about one inch bigger than the present pot. If the roots are coming through the hole in the bottom, it's time to repot.

Mark on your calendar to drain your sprinkling system and disconnect all hoses by the end of October. Even if you have a frost free hydrant, don't leave the hose connected or you might be in for a big mess and a plumber's bill. Good for the plumber but not for the gardener.

A beautiful bulb that's blooming now is the autumn crocus or colchicum. It's lavender and much, much bigger than the ordinary crocus. The variety I have is called "Giant". The leaves come up in spring and then die back in summer. Then in fall, when you have forgotten about them, up shoots the lovely bloom. It is sure to make a dreary flower bed come alive.

Don't waste those fall leaves. Put them through a chipper if you have one and use them for mulch. Or, use them as walkways in a vegetable garden. Or spread them over the vegetable garden to be turned under in spring. Added, chopped, to a compost pile, they make compost by spring. But don't leave them on perennial beds.

It's time to sit back and enjoy the changing colors of the woods, either yours or along the highways. It's time to take stock of all that has happened this past year and good or bad, aren't we thankful to have been a part of this year.

In many instances fall planting of perennials is to be preferred over spring planting. You must, however, do the transplanting early enough to allow plants to become well rooted, or established, before the ground freezes for the winter. A good general rule is that perennials which bloom in early spring benefit by autumn planting, while perennials which bloom in late summer or autumn should be planted in the spring. For the most part, these "rules of thumb" have been observed to be true over many hundreds of years. But remember that all rules of thumb have exceptions. Phlox and Oriental Poppies are best divided shortly after blooming, while Chrysanthemums, Lupines and Anemones must wait until the beginning of warm weather. I guess the best way to plant is to know each plant. My very old gardening book (about 50 years old), which was given to me when I was a young gardener, is my guide if I forget. I like to move or plant as many plants as possible in fall since in spring, everything needs doing and I just don't like to take the time to plant properly. Plus fall planting gets the plants off to a running start next spring.

One little trick that is very beneficial to all your perennials is to arrange soil about the crown, so that water flows away from it. The plant will settle and be injured if a pool of water stands and freezes during winter. In spring, it's best to plant level or even allow a little depression about the stem to catch water.

Occasionally some gardener voices some concerns to me about arranging perennials according to colors and I always tell them what a fine gardener once told me. This is your lot, your house, your yard and your plants. Put them where you like them and use any colors you like or all colors at once. You don't get to choose many things in this life but this choice is yours. Even my perfect Ma had stuff scattered all over the hillside. Her front yard was probably 300 feet and she had a cherry tree, Rose of Sharon, mock orange, peonies and two rock gardens, plus roses here and there. I imagine she originally planted where the soil was best and wherever her mother-in-law before her had not planted. If anyone had ever mentioned to her that there was a right or wrong place to plant, she would have just smiled. Even Pa didn't tell her where to plant. I remember that some wild roses grew on an old wooden fence at the bottom of the long front yard and those roses disturbed Pa. For one thing, he liked to have clean fence rows around the house so little varmints couldn't attract snakes. But when the wild roses were mentioned, she just smiled and that ended that conversation.

If you plant a tree or shrub this fall, consider placing a piece of tile near the roots to help with watering next summer. For the winter, just place a stone over the tile. You will be so pleased with that tile next spring and summer.

If someone offers you some straw-filled manure this fall, consider yourself very lucky and use it as mulch as soon as the ground is frozen solid. Use this around your new trees and shrubs. You might not want to use this mulch around the front door!

If you have had some of your house plants drop their leaves after bringing them inside for the winter, don't worry. Some of the more sensitive ones may drop all or some of their leaves but will grow new ones after they have become acclimated to indoor temps and moisture. One temperamental plant is the ficus. There are many varieties but the most popular one is known as Ficus Benjamina or the Weeping Fig, or sometimes called the Willow Fig. However, once it finds just the right spot in the house, it seems to grow in leaps and bounds and must be trimmed to size. The main reason they don't do well if taken outside is that they require moisture in summer and no direct sunlight. It naturally loses some leaves in winter so if yours is shedding, don't despair, it's natural. All plants in the Ficus family are a bit temperamental.

A little advice about placing your house plants inside: all blooming plants need some sunlight at least part of the day and they need to be turned often for even blooms. During dark winter days, there's little danger of getting too much sun. Ferns, vines and other foliage plants do well in North and East windows but flowers are the result of exposure to South and West windows. There are some plants, such as ivies, which will survive well in rooms without windows but most plants like at least some light.

Don't forget to make arrangements to save your wood ashes this winter. A good way is to keep them over the winter in metal buckets with tight tops stored in some out of the way place. Just storing them in a pile is wasted effort because the potash will leach out in winter rains. Many plants benefit from ashes spread out in beds in spring but the most notable is the aster which really loves potash. Roses and most perennials like a thin layer of ashes.

It is not too late to cut off the blooms of the crape myrtle. In fact, it's the best time. Don't trim the limbs, just cut off to where the flowers started. For those who want to trim their crape myrtles to the appearance of a tree with five or six main trunks, this is also a good time.

As hard as it is to keep things clean in the flower beds, it's a necessary chore at this time. Most of us won't be as enthusiastic as we were last spring but keeping your garden weed free is very important. This is the time most of the noxious weeds go to seed and you will either deal with them now or next spring and summer, ALL spring and summer. A few desperate gardeners will run the lawn mower over the vegetable plot or the beds with annuals only. That is better than nothing. Then there are the tops and leaves that lie on the bed all winter, creating a diseased garden. All the debris has to be gotten out of the flower beds.

If you can, you should plough your vegetable garden now to get off to a great start next spring and it also will allow the soil to warm up faster. Also it turns under all the junk left on the garden, turning it into compost.

We hear a lot about the pesky critters such as raccoons, groundhogs, rabbits, squirrels and most of all, deer. I pass on as much information as I know but there's never anything that deters deer from eating all that grows in the yards. They even come up to eat flowers at the door. Well, I have heard of something that works! A friend says that they had a garden near a storage shed/garage at the back of their property with a garden nearby and deer ate all their vegetables until they heard of an answer. They put a radio in the outbuilding that is on all the time. The deer have not bothered their garden since. The voices and music scare them away. The radio noise is far enough away from the house that it doesn't bother them. It beats the Dial soap which is a disaster since rabbits love the soap and will come hopping from everywhere. There are a lot of other things to hang in trees, none of which seem to work. You might try the radio.

A plant that has become a favorite of mine is ornamental grass. There are many, many kinds with many colors and heights. They are about the toughest plants you can find and are just beautiful about this time in fall. My daughter, who lives next door, can't grow many plants since there are so many roots from the very old trees. But the grass stayed beautiful all summer and doesn't seem to mind the roots. She thinks she will start a new trend in landscaping with all tall grasses rather than the customary foundation plantings. It's her yard, her plants so why not?

You probably have already brought houseplants in for the winter but, just in case you have not, wash them carefully to rid them of all little white flies, etc. before putting them in with your other plants. You can use a garden hose for the large plants. There are insecticides just for houseplants and a can is a good thing to have around. You may have noticed that leaves are dropping from those plants brought indoors. Don't despair. It's just natural with the change of temperature and amount of light.

I remind you to wrap the young newly planted trees in burlap or a paper just for that purpose. They are prone to sun scald and will also get some damage from freezes in winter.

November

Tulips, favorite flowers for centuries, are the last planted of all fall bulbs. Actually, they can be planted from the last of October until the last of November. But if you aren't able to get them in the ground until January, you can still plant them as long as the ground can be worked. If you are thinking of planting tulip bulbs this fall, avoid planting in open windswept places where heavy blooms may be blown apart. They need especially good drainage, adequate moisture and a sunny location, although the Parrot types will stand some shade. If you study the time each tulip starts blooming, you can have a procession of blooms starting in April and going for two months or so.

Many kinds of obsessions with the tulip are interesting. At the peak of the tulipmania, wealthy

Dutch folk bought a single bulb for what was then the equivalent of 15 years annual income of the working class Dutch folk. The French also were obsessed with the tulip during the reign of Louis XIV, when women tucked tulips into their underwear. The more expensive the tulip, the more important the woman. That's obsession!

The devastation of most of Europe during World War II affected the tulip trade. Holland passed a law banning the home sales of tulip bulbs but they did, however, trade 4 million tulip bulbs for arms from the U.S.

Holland still dominates the tulip trade. About 3 million bulbs are planted there each year, and 25,000 acres are used to grow the little beauties in this tiny country.

The biggest reasons for tulips not blooming are over-watering and overfeeding. Tulips take very good care of themselves, so if you give them a good home and don't over-mother them, they will flourish.

One more bit of tulip advice: when growing bulbs in containers, provide plenty of drainage. For continual blooms, mix early, mid, and late bloomers in the same pot. Space bulbs close together, with the larger bulbs lower down. To increase their chances of blooming the following year, remove the bulbs from the containers six weeks after the last bloom. Dry and store in a slightly humid place until returning them to a pot or the ground in late fall. You can then recycle the pot with summer annuals.

Before freezing weather, you can plant some garlic cloves and grow your own garlic. Pick large healthy cloves and plant about 8 inches apart. Cover with straw and wait for spring when they will pop up through the straw and you are in the garlic business. Home grown garlic is so much better.

Don't mulch peonies this fall. Or if you mulch, do it very lightly. Peonies do much better if allowed to freeze.

Birds need water almost as much as food, so place a pan of water near their feeder and take it in periodically to thaw when freezing occurs. They also need grit or sand so mix a little fine poultry grit with sand in a place near their food. Bird watching is such a wonderful winter hobby. Remember that you have to care for them this winter if you want them to work for you next year.

Recently, my gardening buddy brought me several gallons of dried rose petals and tiny roses. I have wished for them to make potpourri and now I have lots. I put them in a tall kitchen garbage bag and used ground orris root, cinnamon sticks and whole cloves and rose and spice oils. Next, I will dry some thin orange slices in the microwave and maybe some lemon rind curls. Sounds great, doesn't it. I'm making it for a bazaar and for gifts for friends and a lot for myself. What would I do without friends? This good friend had collected rose petals for me from her garden and her neighbor's all summer. It was my lucky day when she decided to adopt me a few years ago.

Even if you don't plan to have a compost pile, don't waste your coffee grounds. Save the grounds, filters and all, and when you have a can full, dig a hole in your flower bed, stick them in and cover them. I learned that from an old lady a long time ago. When spring comes, when preparing to plant something, you will notice some very dark, rich soil. That was your coffee grounds. Also, that's where you will find lots of earthworms working away enriching the soil.

"If winter comes, can spring be far behind?" I have heard Ma say these words many, many times. She was always a little sad to see fall and winter. And no wonder! You would be too if you heated with a fireplace bigger than some bathrooms and your big kitchen was heated with a cast iron cook stove many years old. Milking still had to be done and the chickens fed and the eggs gathered even in the coldest weather. But, being Ma, she was philosophical about the cold winter and knew that spring would come eventually. Ma and Pa shared life and its hardships so Pa often milked when the weather was really fierce and he always brought chicken corn from the crib. He also made life as comfortable for her as was possible in their everyday life. Now, don't misunderstand. Ma didn't think her life was hard. After all, it was the only way of life she knew.

Being the little sponge that I was, I picked up on Ma's attitude about winter. The falling leaves aren't as beautiful to me as to others. It just means that winter will be coming and the flowers all gone. But I try to be as philosophical as Ma and think of the brighter side. I won't be spending hours every day doing something to the flower beds and can spend time going through catalogs and reading and all the other things I haven't had time to do all summer.

The lovely seed catalogs will be coming soon and I can spend hours on each one. My father did the same. In fact, he was kind of a joke to his neighboring farmers because he grew so many different varieties of each plant in his big vegetable garden. He dearly loved to see the plants come to fruition. He had always wanted a farm and when he had one, he was a great vegetable grower. We had tomatoes in all colors available and several kinds of green beans, etc. And all because it was fun for him. I remember that he grew several kinds of watermelons and cantaloupes. Surely, gardening is in my genes.

Before the cold winds keep you inside, take one last stroll around the flower beds and I'll bet you will find an iris or perennial that should have been moved. It isn't according to all the gardening rules, but it really isn't too late to move iris and most perennials. The roots will have adequate time to settle before any freeze. Just be sure, when moving at this late season, to give the newly transplanted plant plenty of water and mulch well.

When trimming your roses for the winter, save the branches. They make excellent dog repellents. Though I am a dog lover, I don't appreciate the dogs which are turned out to run at night. I hope this doesn't happen in your neighborhood but it does in mine. The dogs soon learn to respect flower beds after stepping on those thorny rose branches. My dogs don't run through the neighborhood and I don't appreciate having my plants dug or trampled by someone else's dog. I had a problem with my husband's favorite big dog once and placed those stems hither and yon in the beds. He came into the house saying that I should be more careful in cleaning up the rose bed. I had to explain that it was my purpose to keep the beloved pet out of my roses.

If you are looking for a chore on some warm fall day, go out and cut all the "suckers" from around your lilac. Speaking of lilacs, I noticed my lilac blooming on the first day of November. There are several blooms. My one and only lilac has the hardest time making a big splash of blooms in spring and this fall blooming will probably give it another setback. Ah, well, if winter comes, can spring be far behind?

There's not much excitement in gardening in November. In fact, it's downright miserable most days after the middle of the month. I am always grateful to sit inside and plan for next year. Yet there are a few things to consider for the dedicated gardener.

There are those tulip bulbs to get in the ground the last of November, the dwarf fruit trees you have been considering, double check to be sure that all sprayers have been thoroughly washed for storing and zap those dandelions that seem to suddenly appear in fall. A handy little helper is the squirt bottle of weed and grass killer that you can buy at any garden center or hardware.

Then there are the roses to cut back.

The question always comes up about what to do to get a flower bed to have that wonderful dark, loose soil for planting perennials. This is the time to get things together to make that soil that looks so good on television. Did you know that a combination of leaf mold, compost and rotted manure makes the absolute best medium for perennials or any other flowers, for that matter. You have the leaves and it's just a matter of chopping them with a lawn mower and raking them, then you may have some compost ready for next spring and now is the time to get manure from some farmer. Believe me, any farmer would gladly let you get all you want. The chopped leaves mixed with the manure and some compost will be ready for spring. If you don't have compost, by all means make a compost pile through the winter months. I put everything in the compost that I can safely add. Good additives are raw kitchen scraps, egg shells, the old, dead perennial tops and annuals, the stuff from the vacuum cleaner and anything except cooked food, meat scraps and citrus fruit peels. Once, while admiring a house as I passed by several times, I finally noticed that the gardener had three bins of compost in back of a gardening shed. Smart gardener. If you have some compost left over from summer, why not start another bin or pile since you have leaves to use for a starter. Another good reason for getting all leaves off your flower beds is that, left on the bed, they will make a fine place for slugs to overwinter.

Another important chore before winter sets in is to check your perennials to be sure that dirt hasn't washed away from the roots. Those bare roots will kill perennials if they go through the winter like that.

If you happen to be a rhubarb lover, you can force rhubarb in a basement or attic by digging a clump, planting it in a large pot or tub and placing it in a warm place such as beside the furnace or attic chimney. Now, why you would want rhubarb is a mystery to me but as Ma always said, "There's no accounting for taste".

If you are a bargain hunter, as most gardeners are forced to be, you might check with your local farm and garden store or nursery to buy some mulch, peat moss and fertilizer in bags at a real bargain. Some places will even give you any bags with holes in them just to get them off their lot. You can rebag them before taking them home. Also, did you know that all those seeds in the seed racks will be destroyed this fall so why not ask the owner if you can have them? Better than throwing them in the garbage.

Did you know that you can plant tulips in those large pots which contained annuals this summer? One pot can hold a dozen or so and what a nice bit of color for next spring. Another use for those pots of dirt is to plant some small evergreens. Then in spring, you can place the pots in the flower beds among perennials until they are big enough for planting elsewhere.

Thanksgiving Day, with turkey, duck, old hen or whatever your family tradition might be, was once quite different for folks who lived near what is now government land. It was customary to take that old blunderbus and go a' hunting for a big turkey for the table.

As you no doubt know, our traditional Thanksgiving meal does not resemble the original Thanksgiving. Hopefully, the only resemblance is the grateful hearts gathered around the table.

This is a great time to go over your garden, while there's a semblance of a garden, and make a list of the things you would like to add., whether it's some beautiful rocks, plants, as garden bench or maybe a statue. This is the time because you can add something to your Christmas list. All the garden catalogs will send a gift certificate. Your local nursery would also be happy to mail a gift certificate. I have never met a gardener who didn't have a wish list, secret or not. Now here's the fun part. Go through books, magazines, catalogs and look at pictures of other gardens. A wish list gives you a place to put down those ideas so you can remember them when it's time to actually lay out a plan.

Next to the needs list, start writing down all the fun ideas that come to mind. Did you always want an herb garden or, maybe a rock garden? Just add them to the list. I know a gardener who gathered big rocks for a rock garden for her mother-in-law. What a neat gift idea! Maybe you always wanted some fruit trees or a cutting garden so you can have all the fresh flowers you want. How about plants to attract birds or some area to attract butterflies? Or maybe you'd like a white and silver garden near your deck for night beauty? I always thought about a real true Colonial garden with vegetables next to flowers. The possibilities are endless.

Now, the real planning may take place over the entire winter, with lists and pictures and books and magazines. Just prop your feet up and let your imagination run wild. All these ideas could be possibilities for next year.

A really good gardening book is "Burpee Complete Gardener" which is a comprehensive, up-to-date, illustrated reference. It's probably the nicest gardening book I own and I use it often. Just drop a hint. It's a MacMillan book so should be easy to find. If you have a problem finding it, contact Burpee.

Pretty soon, after several really cold nights, it will be time to put your roses to bed. But in the meantime, you could remove all the leaves on the lower part so you can see the stems. You can cut off any weak or spindly stems now. You want to leave at least five good, strong stems for each rose. You can do that now. That gives you a head start on the cutting back process for later when it's cold.

While you're out doing a few chores, lay your garden hose down in the foundation plantings and let it run until the ground won't soak up any more water.

You can have a little fun by propagating forsythia, pussy willow, spirea and quince this fall. Take a 12 inch cutting after the plants have dropped their leaves, dip the ends in rooting hormone, such as Rootone, and plant them about 8 inches deep in a trench. Keep the soil moist and when spring comes, put them into containers and keep them at least till fall to plant in a permanent place.

When we think that the beginning of November is going to give us a respite from gardening, along comes these beautiful warm days when we can finish putting the perennials to bed for the winter. By now most all plants have wilted and are ready to cut back. I always leave a few inches to let me locate each plant next spring. Over planting is a real problem in perennial gardens. That is one of the reasons it's such a good idea to have plant markers.

Have you noticed how beautiful nandinas are? It's a wonderful plant if you want to add some real color and pizzazz to a foundation planting or just an addition to any part of the garden. As a specimen planting, be sure to plant three. In summer they have bronze tipped leaves and then small white flowers which become red berries in fall. It has many assets, including the fact that they have no pests and require no spraying. They will grow in full sun or part shade and will grow in poor soil but really prefer a rich, slightly acid soil. They will really put on a show for you with so little attention. They will be bushier if given a pruning and the way to prune them is to think of a pyramid. Make the first cutting to the ground, the next cutting about a foot up and so on to the top. The best time to prune is about the end of November and how convenient that they make such nice winter indoor decoration. A large bowl with some branches containing the berries makes a great centerpiece. Added to a wreath, they are spectacular and they make a great mantle decoration. Since they can't be pruned in summer, why not make this pruning of nandinas the last chore in the winter? Some smart gardener is going to read this column and know that yellow berried nandinas do exist but they are really a freak or a misfit. Some years nandina berries will be a light red and some years, they are maroon. Incidentally, if you want to be correct, the plural is also nandina. This lovely plant which is reminiscent of a bamboo plant is from China or Japan. It's a broadleaf evergreen and can be quite expensive if you buy four year old plants. However, you can buy younger plants and wait. One side benefit is that they multiply and you can dig up the sprouts for another place. I dug up three small plants this summer and now they are about 2 feet tall. I added manure which I buy, the shame of it! What Pa would think if he knew I BOUGHT manure!

You can shape up the Rose of Sharon bush now. It's also a good idea to hill up the soil around the butterfly bush.

If you are thinking of buying a live Christmas tree this year, plan now on where to put it and dig the hole. When you are ready to plant it after Christmas, digging a hole in frozen ground is a big chore. You must get it in the ground immediately after Christmas. It should be in the house no longer than two weeks.

If, while you are cleaning up the flower beds, you find a perennial which you wish you had moved, it's really not too late. Just remember all the rules for replanting any time. Deep hole, water thoroughly before planting and put the plant in its new hole immediately after digging. No letting it lie for an hour or two. If plants have plenty of water to help establish a root system and if they have a little time before a hard freeze, they will be OK.

After the first hard frost, usually in early November, trim your roses back to 12 to 18 inches. Some growers say that 24 inches is enough; others say to prune to 8 inches. I have found that about 18 inches works for me. About the middle of March, or on St. Patrick's Day as an old friend used to claim, they will need pruning again to trim off some dead ends. The idea of trimming them back in November is to cut off enough stems that the wind won't whip them back and forth and destroy the tiny feeder roots.

Sadly, no matter how much time and effort you spend on your roses this fall, some will die. It is very hard to grow white roses and the yellow ones are the next most difficult. Don't ask me why. Just is! You will find that the miniature roses are the hardiest and rarely die out in winter. In fact, I have never lost one. Also they are the easiest to start under fruit jars, my favorite method of propagating. After the ground has begun to freeze, usually when the temperature drops to around 20 degrees for several nights, mound up dirt around the rose plant, up to and above the graft. Get your dirt from some other part of the garden since digging around the rose will damage the tiny roots. So that's the reason you should have a pile of dirt near each rose early in fall. It's not too late to get that pile of dirt ready while it's not too cold. If you still have leaves to rake, consider this way to dispose of them. Pack them loosely in large plastic lawn bags, punch a few holes in the plastic, and fold the tops over to secure them with a brick. The leaves will decompose in 6 to 12 months and your leaf mold will be ready for the compost heap.

If you're thinking of buying a live tree for Christmas, decide where you want to plant it after Christmas and dig the hole now since the ground will likely be frozen by January when you want to plant outside. It's very important to get that tree outside in the ground as soon as possible after Christmas. It should be in the house no longer than two weeks.

After the first hard frost, usually in early November, trim your roses back to 12 to 18 inches. Some growers say that 24 inches is enough; others say to prune to 8 inches. I have found that about 12 inches works for me. About the middle of March or on St. Patrick's Day, as an old friend used to claim, they will need pruning again to trim off some dead ends. The idea of trimming them back in November is to cut off enough stems that the wind won't whip them back and forth and destroy the tiny feeder roots.

Sadly, no matter how much time you spend on your roses this fall, some will die. It is very hard to grow white roses and the yellow ones are the next most difficult. Don't ask me why. Just is!

You will find that the miniature roses are the hardiest and rarely die out in winter. In fact, I have never lost one. Also they are easiest to start under fruit jars, my favorite method of propagating.

After the ground has begun to freeze, usually when the temperature drops to around 20 degrees for several nights, mound up dirt around the rose plant, up to and above the graft. Get your dirt from some other part of the garden since digging around the rose will damage the roots. So that's the reason you should have a pile of dirt near each rose early in the fall. It's not too late to get that pile of dirt ready while it's not so cold.

December

As we grow older, or perhaps it's better stated, as I grow older, each year I spend more time thinking of Christmases of long ago. I seem to go farther back each year. I hope you will bear with me while I tell you what Christmas was like at our house more than 60 years ago. My mother, as we all are inclined to do, always wanted to "go home" for Christmas at her parents' home, my Ma and Pa. Mama and Daddy gathered their three little girls, all the packages tucked securely and secretly in the trunk of the '37 Chevrolet and off we went from Canton to Lyon County for Christmas. It was so important to me to be at Ma and Pa's because they had the big fireplaces for Santa Claus. Maybe you had a Ma and Pa with the big fireplace.

My earlier memories include the annual "picking of the Christmas Cedar tree". Until I was seven, I lived near Ma and Pa and Ma and I made several forays into the back pasture looking for a tree that was just right. We searched the rocky hillside for just the right tree and about the middle of December, we made a trip to cut the tree. Ma kept the Christmas tree on the big dining room table in a big bucket of sand with tissue paper all around and it stayed there until the "Big Day" when it was removed to another place. My dear Ma had few things to trim the tree but those few were angels with silky long white hair and a few baubles which were all very old. How I wish I had those things today. I have always thought those decorations the most beautiful in the world. She loved the icicles when they first came on the market and the artificial snow which made me itch for a day.

Ma cooked enough cakes and pies to feed the whole neighborhood. It was necessary because their kin came from all around sometime during the Holidays. She had her own turkeys, ducks and old hens and roosters plus hams from their smokehouse. Also she had big jars of canned vegetables of all kinds and her pickles, preserves, canned wild plums, blackberries and the hickory nuts, walnuts and hazelnuts. Then there was the orchard from which she canned apples, pears, cherries and peaches. Altogether, Ma set a fine table which was known far and wide in her little community. She made the most marvelous Lord and Lady Baltimore cakes plus orange and pineapple cakes and several others. The greatest of all, and Ma's masterpiece, was a great white cake iced with white seven-minute icing and fresh grated coconut.

There was a smell in Ma's old house which I have never known anywhere else. Maybe it was the Christmas smells of all the years because the old house was built long before the Civil War and had seen many Lewises and Halls celebrate Christmas.

Now Ma and Pa didn't have many grandchildren and they were very permissive. We always had at least one dog and one cat that we refused to leave behind so Ma had to cope with our animals. Ma was very nice about the dog but just barely tolerated our old cat, Dude, especially since Dude was not a very mannerly cat at her house which was strange to him.

After we moved away from the farm, we would arrive, cat and/or dog in tow with all in high spirits. I always thought Ma's house looked prettier than any other place on earth with her little tree and the big pie safe all full of cakes and pies and that cedar smell all over the house. With the big back log burning in the fireplace and all those good smells and the Christmas tree, it felt like Christmas.

On Christmas morning, we rushed into the big room where our stockings were hung and where the gifts were piled up in three separate piles for each of us. We, as all children then, were not pampered with many gifts. We usually got one big gift and maybe a few others with a sock full of fruit, candy and nuts. But, oh how excited we were! After all the excitement began to die down, our uncle from Evansville might come with his daughter who was our age. And the

"Uncle" who lived on Pa's farm would come with his wife and their grown son. Sometimes one of Pa's relatives, with family, might also come. But never fear, Ma was well prepared. She had a huge table in the kitchen where she fed all the children first, that being one of her very important rules. We never had to wait for the adults to finish. There might be more than one table of adults and THEY might have to wait but never the children.

My grandmother was a bustling little woman. She actually was not very fast in her movements but always seemed to bustle. She was a very beautiful woman with the fairest skin with a pink tinge and the bluest eyes, and as far back as I remember, she had white hair, which she pulled back into a bun on the back of her neck. Even into her eighties, she had no wrinkles or blemishes and she credited her skin to her big hats and long sleeves.

All that wonderful food lasted for several days and what a good time we all had. The men folk would often get up a game of "Sell Pitch", a card game favored by all, and the women would finish cleaning the kitchen and go into another room for a gossip fest. I was hard put to choose which place to be.

As we all know, not all Christmases are happy times. I have some memories of some very traumatic times. Looking back on them from many years, they seem funny now but not so then.

About the most traumatic Christmas for me was the time our neighbor shot Santa Claus. My father had a tenant on his farm that was just one big headache and he finally did himself in at Christmas. I was in the first grade and walked to a little country school with the children of this soon to become infamous man. As we were walking home from school in mid-December, I asked the little girl what Santa would bring her and she sadly said, "He ain't gonna come this year. Daddy shot im out behind the smokehouse cause I heered the shotgun." I finally reached home and rushed into the house screaming and crying to tell Daddy that Mr. Name Withheld had shot Santa. What worse thing could happen in this big wide world? When Daddy finally got the whole story, he was very reassuring and convinced me that Santa was alive and well but even as young as I was, I knew from Daddy's dark looks that his tenant was in for a bad time. To tell you what kind of man my father was, he went to town to buy some toys and candy for those children and took them to them on Christmas morning. Looking back, I feel so sorry for those children.

The next most traumatic Christmas was when the mail carrier deliberately gave our Sears package to me, six years old, at school. He had to pass up our mail box to go on to the school and then he gave the torn package to me. There was my sister's and my little piggy banks and two dolls. My mother or father had gone each morning to watch for Mr. Rogers' car so that they could get the packages first and hide them. All these years later, I think Mr. Rogers epitomized cruelty.

Then there was the fiasco of my first really pretty doll. This doll was all the things any little girl could want. It had long blond curls and was dressed in an organdy dress and bonnet with lacy petticoats. Now the kicker in this story is that this doll had a crier in her back and cried when she was put on her back. My little sister and her friend thought this a great marvel and cut her open to see what this crier looked like. Of course, out came all kinds of stuffing and my doll was ruined forever as far as I could see. That was my last doll but was no big loss because I had really wanted a football.

Then the football story comes next. The following Christmas when I was probably ten, I got that wondrous football. It lasted all of a week and was burst and ruined by my cousin of about sixteen. Sadly, I never got another. By this time, I had other wants including jewelry and clothes.

I never looked back on these little events as ruining my Christmases however. They were happy times anyway.

Eventually I had a family of my own and vowed to see that these things didn't happen to them. But alas, they happen in all families. Once, my husband and two boys went to the woods to get a live tree. They came back with a tree too tall for even our tall ceilings. We finally cut it to fit but it filled the old hall. We decorated it and put lights on it and what a glorious thing it was. One night we heard an awful racket and rushed to see what it was. Our big Tiger cat had climbed up into the tree looking for the bird smell and found an old nest. He had turned the tree over and there on the floor lay the tree, surrounded by broken decorations. We finally righted the tree, salvaged most of the decorations, found and soothed Tiger and tied the tree to the ceiling. All of us look back on that event as terribly funny.

One Christmas event seemed funny to all in our family except my mother. We were all at Ma's house as usual for Christmas. The big day came and Mama was preparing the turkey for the oven. There were a lot of things to cook in the oven and a great idea struck her. Why not use Ma's new big pressure canner? It would certainly hold that great bird and save all those hours in the oven. So out came the canner, in went the bird and Mama set the timer. The problem was that Mama knew nothing about that big canner and had too quickly scanned the directions. When the canner had cooled, she removed the top and lo, all the meat had fallen off the turkey and there was the naked carcass. My father and Ma assured her that the meat was wondrously tender and was just fine. But that was always a sore spot for Mama. Never again did she try a shortcut in cooking the Christmas turkey.

These are some of my memories of Christmases past and I hope you have enjoyed a trip down memory lane with me.

❀   ❀   ❀   ❀

Isn't it a wonderful coincidence that the very time you want some greenery for the house is the time that it's best to trim some evergreens. You can make sprays or wreaths with your own greenery. For wreaths, spruces, pines, hollies, arborvitaes and cypresses all work well wound around a grapevine base. You can even throw in some of the broadleaf evergreens such as rhododendrons or boxwood. You just need a base of grapevine and some florist's wire. Barberries are at their best now also. Magnolia makes the best greenery of all whether it's your own or you con a neighbor out of some. The American holly is probably my favorite plant for greenery, especially after it gets old enough to have red berries. If you are thinking of planting one, be sure to plant it far enough from the house to allow for its growth because they get very large.

When you are ready to take down the tree and put away the ornaments, you may wonder what to do with the tree if it's a real tree. Here in LBL country we can take it to the lake to be placed in the lake as a hiding place for the game fish. If you don't choose to do that, you can cut off the branches and use them for additional protection for perennials. Or, put the tree next to a backyard fence for shelter for the birds during snows. Or, put bird food on the branches. You can put pine cones with peanut butter and seeds on the branches or buy the packets already made up for hanging food. You'll feel better recycling that tree. If you have an artificial tree, you have to go through the same old chore of taking it down. Why not do as a friend once did and leave it up till June and by then, she thought Christmas was too near to take it down and just put it up again.

We like to think that all our carefully purchased gifts will be appreciated and that we wait anxiously for the snow falling softly on Christmas Eve and all the family happy and well. And we know it isn't always so. There's the guest who comes with a dog that is unwelcome and poorly trained or the grandchildren who bring their cat. There's the time your own cat ate the tinsel and had a quick trip to the vet. Cats always want to eat tinsel, you know. If there are several children in the family, someone is bound to get sick at Christmas.

There was the time my mother sent gifts to my sister in Ohio intended for me in Minnesota and vice versa. Everyone enjoyed that except my poor mother.

When we all look back on Christmases past, we look through rose-tinted glasses. I forget the miserable visits of the cousins and aunts and uncles who did me out of my bed and all other unpleasantness. They always seemed to get my favorite pieces of fried chicken, an unforgivable thing in my young life. There was the cousin who was a miserable little city sissy who was afraid of the feather duster and whom we conned into thinking the red cow gave white milk and the Jersey gave chocolate. How we tried to make his visit his worst nightmare.

December

I just remember the crisp, cold nights and lying in bed with my sister Sally, listening so hard for the sound of the sleigh bells and possibly little hooves clattering on the old tin roof and I think of the old poem:

> *Backward, turn backward*
> *Oh time in your flight.*
> *Make me a child again*
> *Just for tonight.*